BISTRO
Pizza
AT HOME

BISTRO Pizza AT HOME

130 Pizza & Flatbread Recipes

Lloyd Sittser

⊞ WILLOW CREEK PRESS®

Published by Willow Creek Press
P.O. Box 147, Minocqua, Wisconsin 54548

For information on other Willow Creek Press titles,
call 1-800-850-9453

Printed in Canada

Contents

Introduction

Coast to coast, innovative bistros are booming in the USA. Bistros are upbeat fun establishments with good vibrations and active ambience. Much of bistros appeal lies in their relaxed dress codes and lack of pretensions, where you can leave your hair up or let it down. They are attracting a loyal patronage with their friendly service and moderate prices.

Bistros are offering their guests flexible menus and delicious food. Sure, the neighborhood pizza joint is known for pizza. Yet everyone seems to accept that the truly special pizza will be found at the local bistro. That's where one can expect to find a gifted and creative chef. These talented chefs are no longer content to limit themselves exclusively to traditional pizza toppings.

Popular today on the bistro menu are specialty gourmet pizzas. These specialty pizzas are designed with seductive visual appeal to enhance the pizzas presentation. Whether called Designer, Specialty or Gourmet pizza, they are all Bistro pizza. Chef creativity with a variety of premium non-traditional toppings is the expectation. Bistros may feature their favorites as signature pizzas to promote as special to their establishment. These pizzas will titillate and tantalize your taste buds for a memorable dining experience.

During the 90's I begin experimenting with specialty pizzas to add to my menu at my former pub, Cassidy's Pub Extraordinaire in Manhattan Beach, California. Pizza development has continued for an advanced version of Cassidy's Pub named Bistro Rocks www.bistrorocks.com. The Pizza recipes in this book are the product of those experiments.

Bistro Rocks features an exhibition kitchen with a hearth pizza oven with Old World charm. It is centralized behind a hip counter/bar configuration ideal for grazing and socializing. With the kitchen stage set for entertainment the room transforms into theater. The bistro stars are the pizzaioli pizza prepping and performing for the patron's entertainment. This concept is often mirrored in thousands of homes where family and friends gather around the kitchen counter to party and share pizza. Now you can add your own specialty signature pizza to the party, whether it is a communal party or a party of one. It is Show Time and now you are the star!

Pizza History

Long before the first pizza was assembled, the ancient Egyptians were rolling out the dough. The Greeks learned from these accomplished bakers and shared their bread baking expertise with the Romans. The Roman invaders introduced the French to flat breads. The French tossed some onion, garlic and anchovies on them and voilà, pissaladiere. This flat bread creation is still on the pizza menu today in many bistros. The foundation for pizza had been created.

Water buffalo were imported from India to the Campania region of what is now Italy in the 7th century AD. With them the production of mozzarella cheese was established. Another important step towards the creation of pizza had been realized. Today most mozzarella is produced from cow's milk.

The tomato originated in South America and migrated to Central America and Mexico. It wasn't introduced to the American colonies and the Old World until the exploration of Peru and Mexico by Spanish explorers. Initially people in the North American colonies and England feared the tomato poisonous. Apparently it didn't matter that when they discovered the tomato the local inhabitants were eating them, con gusto. The plant initially was used mainly for decorative purposes. Once the citizenry realized the tomato was safe for consumption the culinary appreciation for the tomato was assured. The future was now rosy for red sauce! The Spanish had tomatoes on the menu by the early 1600s. In Naples a cookbook with tomato recipes was published in 1692. All the ingredients for pizza were now available. It was only a matter of time until some hungry soul would toss some cheese and a tomato on a flatbread. Pizza had arrived!

By the 19th century pizza could be purchased from fixed stands in Naples. The pizzaioli would assemble the pizza on a counter. Customers could select from popular toppings offered at that time, oil, cheese, basil, oregano, mushrooms, proscuitto, garlic and anchovies. To transport the pizza from the hot ovens directly to the populace some venders used metal boxes with vented lids. Others would walk the streets of Naples displaying their pizzas on cutting boards, ready to be sliced and sold. Now you could enjoy pizza on the go and we have been running with it ever since.

The first real pizzeria opened in Naples around 1830. In 1889 Raffaele Esposito, proprietor of a well known pizzeria, presented several pizzas to Italian Queen Margherita di Savoia. She selected as her favorite one with tomato, fresh mozzarella and basil. He named it Margherita in her honor. Today you may order Pizza Margherita at your corner bistro. Signor Antonio had set the table for pizza development.

Pizza appeared in America around the end of the 19th century with the immigration of Neapolitans. In 1905, Lombardi's became the first licensed pizzeria in the USA. It opened in the Little Italy section of New York City. Initially pizza was served with imported San Marzano tomatoes, fresh mozzarella, basil and garlic. Eventually other toppings such as sausage, peppers, onions and anchovies were added. It was cooked in a coal oven and produced a light thin and crispy pizza. New York style pizza was established.

In 1943 the Allied armies landed on the Italian mainland liberating and occupying Italy. During the occupation many appreciative soldiers were introduced to pizza for the first time. At the end of the Second World War many returned home wanting more. During the war deep dish pizzas were being developed and served by pizzerias in Chicago. The GI's returning to Chicago were welcomed to the communal table. Deep dish pizza joined America's favorite pizzas.

In the 1980s West Coast restaurateurs were experimenting with light, thin crust, individual size pizzas. The toppings were non-traditional, fresh and healthy and some considered exotic. These eclectic pizzas fused a variety of ethnic cuisine into taste sensations worthy of indulging. Some traditionalists may protest the authenticity of these pizzas, but purity is for the soul, not pizza! This style of pizza became known as California Pizza and its popularity has been established nationwide.

Today pizza is the world's favorite pie. Due to war, migration, communication, curiosity, rapid advances in technology and increased tourism pizza has blasted off. It has been flying high ever since.

The evolution of pizza continues. Bistro and home chefs are rising to the challenge with creativity and their eye on the pie. Bistro Pizza can now be savored everywhere, whether regional, New York, Chicago or California style.

Pizza is perfect for partaking at home or on the go. It is fun finger food best enjoyed in communal camaraderie. Socialize and share it with your family and friends. It can also be enjoyed alone or with your favorite pet. I shared numerous pizzas with my little dog Rags who is my greatest pizza fan and taster. Yes she loved them all! Realistically it is to be assumed the readers will not be as appreciative of each and every recipe in this book as she was. Select those that appeal to your taste preferences to perfect your pizza making skills.

Pizza is tasty, nutritious, filling and affordable. It appeals to all ages. Research has shown Lycopene, an antioxidant found in tomatoes to be especially beneficial nutritionally when cooked in a pizza or pasta sauce. It may help keep arteries young and increases prostate health in men. Tomatoes are also a source of vitamin A and C, folate and potassium. Cheese is high in protein and calcium and a good source of vitamin B12. Some aged cheeses may even help prevent tooth decay. Research continues.

There are many sincerely dedicated restaurateurs and inviting dining establishments. They work diligently to provide their customers delicious food with warm hospitality.

Salutations to them and they deserve to be rewarded with our appreciation and patronage. Unfortunately to our dismay there are a few exceptions. Not all restaurateurs are as conscientious or dedicated. You may have hungrily waited for your pizza only to be left with the taste of sour grapes. Now with the help of this book you can roll out the dough and bistro chefs beware. You can create tasty bistro style pizza whenever you feel adventurous. You will find pizza fun making and baking. Be adventurous and take it to the limit!

Many ingredients and toppings can be purchased already processed or they can be prepped a day in advance when necessary. With a little inspiration and experimentation you will achieve the perfect balance of toppings and flavors.

Now it is time to party and eat hearty. Invite your friends and fellow pizza connoisseurs for a special bistro style treat. Create a fun informal bistro atmosphere. Display your specialty toppings on the counter. Preheat your oven. Open your bistro and check the ties at the door. Wow the hungry with your pizza expertise and creativity. Throw some corn meal on the peel and slap on a dough round. Encourage your guests to top it and design their own specialty bistro pizza. Make it personal, it is their signature bistro pizza. Now it is Show Time! Peel it, bake it and display it! The evolution of pizza continues.

Bon appétit!

1

2

3

4

5

6

7

8

9

Pizza Equipment & Utensils

You may already have in your kitchen most of the implements used to make pizza. Not all of these listed will be necessary for you to have to produce excellent pizza. A scale for weighing ingredients, a pizza (baking) stone and pizza peel can prove especially beneficial in producing bistro quality pizza. You can knead the dough by hand or use your mixer of choice. I prefer an upright mixer but you can attain similar results using alternative methods.

1. **Upright Mixer with Dough Hook.** Use it to mix and knead dough.

2. **Food Processor.** Use it to mix and knead dough.

3. **Pizza (Baking) Stone.** Use it to bake your pizza on. It will absorb moisture and crisp your pizza crust while baking. Pre-heat the stone on high heat for one hour in advance of baking the pizza.

   Cornmeal Brush. Use it to brush cornmeal off the hot pizza stone when baking multiple pizzas. If you are only baking a limited number of pizzas the brush may not be necessary.

4. **Pizza (Bakers) Peel.** Use it to transfer your pizza onto the pizza stone and extract it after baking. Wooden peels with beveled edges and metal peels are available. I prefer using a wooden peel to transport the pizza onto the stone, and a metal one to extract the pizza off the stone. Select a peel that works best for you. Sprinkle corn meal on the peel, place the pizza round on it and top your pizza.

5. **Wire Rack.** Use it to rest your pizza on after baking. It will help to maintain a crispy crust and prevent a soggy bottom.

   Bread Knife. Use it to portion the pizza dough and for slicing deep dish pizzas.

   Chefs Knife. Use it to slice and dice your pizza toppings.

6. **Pizza Screen.** Use it to assemble your pizza on and provide support while baking. The holes in the screen will allow the bottom of the dough to bake and produce a crispier crust. You can use a pizza screen if you do not have a baking stone or pizza peel.

   Pizza Slicing Wheel. Use it to portion your pizza into individual slices.

   Measuring Cups. Use them to measure the ingredients.

   Oven Thermometer. Use it to gauge the oven temperature.

Basting Brush. Use it to brush vegetable toppings and dough rounds with garlic herb oil prior to baking.

Measuring Spoons. Use them to measure small quantities.

Ladles (2, 3 and 4 ounce). Use them to portion and spread sauce.

7. **Tart Pan with Removable Bottom (10–12 inch).** Use it to bake deep dish pizza. You can substitute it with a deep dish pizza pan.

Grilling Iron. Use it to grill vegetables and fruit. It can also be used in place of a wire rack to rest the baked pizza on.

Pizza Server with Elevators. Use it to prevent condensation absorption into the crust after baking and help prevent soggy bottom.

8. **Non Reactive Stainless Steel Bowls.** Use them to activate yeast in and to ferment dough in. You can substitute them with glass bowls.

Plastic Bowls. Use them to retard dough balls in.

Cheese Grater. Use it to shred and grate cheese. Do not use for fresh mozzarella (you can use an egg slicer or sharp knife for fresh mozzarella).

9. **Scale.** Use it to weigh your dough ingredients and toppings.

Cornmeal. Use on the pizza peel to facilitate the transfer of the pizza onto the pizza stone

Rolling Pin. Use it to roll out your pizza dough if you wish a thin cracker style crust. Select a sturdy hard wood pin at least 12 inches long.

Utensils Not Illustrated

Thermometer. Use it to determine the water temperature for activating the yeast and checking the dough temperature.

Thin Crust Pizza Pan. Use it to bake your pizza on when a pizza stone and peel or screen are not available.

Deep Dish Pizza Pan. Use it to bake deep dish Chicago style pizza.

Egg Slicer. Use it to slice fresh mozzarella.

Pizza Dough Ingredients

Flour

To create your bistro pizza you will need to formulate a reliable delicious foundation for your toppings. First you will need to select flour that provides you the baking results that you are looking for. If you are looking for a whiter pizza crust you should select bleached flour. If you prefer a noticeably creamier yellow appearance you should select unbleached flour. Both bleached and unbleached flour will process the same except for their color development.

You can not control the production of the flour, but you can your selection. Fluctuating yearly weather conditions will affect the moisture content of wheat and flour resulting in some inconsistency. The milling process and wheat variety will also contribute to inconsistency. Millers can compensate for these variables by mixing and blending wheat and flour. Flour is produced by millers grinding and sifting the seeds of cereals. Wheat flour (also known as white flour) is the primary flour used in pizza dough. It is finely ground from the starchy endosperm of the wheat kernel. Whole wheat flour is produced by including the bran and germ with the endosperm in the milling process.

Protein is the primary strengthening factor in flour. The protein content of flour relates to the hardness of the wheat kernel. A hard wheat kernel will produce higher protein content. Flour with moderate-to-high protein content is used in pizza dough. High protein flour maximizes moisture retention for retarding dough (storing under refrigeration) and is more tolerant to mixing and shaping. It will affect the shrinkage and stretch while forming and how crispy the end product will be. Protein content affects the durability of dough and gives pizza crust its bite. The lower the protein content the tenderer the bite. The higher the protein content the crispier and chewier the bite.

Food service professionals like to know the protein content in flour. They can request spec sheets from suppliers and manufacturers that usually are unavailable to the general public. The protein content of flour is rarely indicated on the flour package, and the protein listed under Nutrition Facts isn't relevant. If you shop around you will find that some baking catalogue companies will print the protein content for their flour in their catalogues.

"All purpose flour" with a protein content of 10–12% is preferred for deep dish pizza. "Bread flour" with a protein content of 12–13% is often used for thin crust pizza. "High gluten flour" with a protein content of 13–14% is frequently used for New York style thin crust pizza. It is best kneaded with a mixer to fully develop its gluten

It is not imperative to determine the protein level for your flour selection. For thin crust pizza most premium quality "bread flour" will produce excellent results. Use premium "all purpose flour" for deep dish pizza. Organic flour is available for the health conscious if that is your preference.

Try experimenting with different flour brands and select the one that rises to your high expectations. Note the particular characteristics of each flour brand you experiment with. Be sure to write them down for future reference. After experimenting with various flour brands I selected King Arthur Flour and Bobs Red Mill for consistent good results. The thin crust pizzas in this book were created with "unbleached bread flour" with a protein content of 12.7%. "Unbleached all purpose flour" with a protein content of 11.7% was used for the deep dish pizza dough.

Olive Oil

Oil is optional in your pizza dough and you can omit it if you are concerned about your fat intake. When used in dough oil lubricates gluten increasing tenderness and moistness. It assists in color development. It will add richness to the dough and make it easier to handle. It decreases snapback and lessens tearing of the dough during shaping. If you follow the pizza dough recipes you will be within the recommended oil content of 3% of total flour weight for thin crust pizza dough. For deep dish pizza you can increase the amount of oil. When you add extra oil you should decrease the water content by 50% of the total extra oil weight. Brush a tablespoon of oil over the dough round prior to baking and it will add flavor and help prevent a doughy/gummy layer forming.

Salt

Salt acts as a flavor enhancer and plays a role in fermentation. If you are concerned about your salt intake it is better to eliminate it on your toppings rather than in your dough. Salt will strengthen your dough and provide rise during baking. As you increase the percentage of salt the fermentation rate will gradually slow.

Sweeteners, Honey and Sugar

Sweeteners assist in fermentation and enhance flavor. They aid bread's color development, tenderness and moisture. Used minimally in pizza dough they are optional and you can omit them if concerned about your caloric intake.

Water

Your cities water should have sufficient hardness for good dough development. Medium-hard water is preferable for baking. Soft water has a weakening affect on dough making it stickier and harder to handle. If you feel your water deficient try substituting bottled water.

Yeast

Yeast will contribute flavor, aroma, texture and manageability to your dough. When you use yeast in dough it metabolizes honey or sugar to produce carbon dioxide gas. Allowing the dough to ferment will produce a crust that is less starchy and have more full-bodied flavor. Fermentation takes place when the gas is trapped inside the dough. As the gas expands it will cause your dough to rise and produce a lighter airy crust.

There are three types of yeast that can be used in pizza dough. When used correctly they will produce similar results. Select one that fits your specifications. Some may prefer the flavor of compressed yeast and others the consistency of active dry or instant yeast.

Instant Dry Yeast is my preference and can be added directly into the flour mix with the other dry ingredients.

Active Dry Yeast should be hydrated in a bowl of warm water at 105–110°. Yeast responds to temperature and starts to react to heat stress at 115° and will die at 140°. If you add a small amount of honey or sugar it will help facilitate yeast development. Allow the yeast to hydrate in a bowl with honey or sugar and water for 10 minutes. That will evenly disperse the yeast and achieve consistent performance. For best results you should not hydrate active dry yeast at a colder temperature, or for a longer period of time. If the yeast does not activate and create surface foam on the water it is defective and you should replace it.

Compressed Yeast (known as fresh or wet) can be crumbled directly into the dough mixture. It should be kept refrigerated and used within a month.

You can use this formula for yeast substitutions: 100 parts of compressed yeast = 50 parts of active dry yeast = 33 parts of instant dry yeast, or 1–1/2–1/3.

You can get excellent results fermenting your dough at normal room temperature. The speed of fermentation can be increased by raising the environmental temperature and/or increasing the level of sweeteners in your dough.

Refrigerate Compressed Yeast at all times and Dry Yeast after opening.

Proofing Active Dry Yeast

1. Add 1 teaspoon honey to 10–11 ounces of 110° water and stir.
2. Add 2 teaspoons Active Dry Yeast to the water and honey blend to proof for 10 minutes.
3. Yeast after activation and proofing 10 minutes.
4. Pour the proofed yeast into a food processor bowl and mix with the dry ingredients or -
5. Pour the proofed yeast into an upright mixers bowl for mixing with the dry ingredients.
6. Proofed yeast added to the dry ingredients in an upright mixers bowl and ready to mix.

Pizza Dough—What You Should Know

Bakers Percentages—Optional information for serious pizzaioli (pizza cooks).

You can create your own dough recipe using "baker's percentages." You will need to multiply each individual ingredient by the flour weight. First you must determine the desired amount of flour for the recipe (for example 18 ounces flour = 100%). For a desired 60% water percentage the formula would be .60 × 18 = 10.8 ounces. Next you will multiply the remaining individual ingredients percentage by the flour. For example if you want 3% oil in your dough recipe the formula is .03 × 18 = .54 ounces.

You may also want to determine the percentage of various dough ingredients in an existing dough recipe. To do so you will divide the weight of each ingredient individually by the weight of the flour. For example if the recipe calls for 11 ounces water and the flour in the recipe weighs 18 ounces, the formula is 11 ÷ 18 = 61%.

Portioning, Weighing and Measuring

Baking is more exacting than many other methods of cooking. It requires more precise ingredient portioning, measuring and weighing. It is preferable you weigh recipe ingredients for accuracy but when you are working with small amounts it is not always practical. You may prefer using a combination of weighing and measuring. You can weigh the larger amounts like flour and water. For smaller amounts such as yeast, salt and olive oil you can use measuring spoons.

Each ingredient in your dough will interact with the others positively or negatively. You should take care in portioning and mixing ingredients to achieve balance. If not in balance your dough may become too tough or too soft. After you mix the dough it should be satiny smooth. Barely tacky is acceptable but not sticky to touch.

Increasing or decreasing the water content in the dough recipes will impact your dough's characteristics. Experiment with your flour selection to establish your preferred flour to water ratio. Weigh your flour and water individually and take notes for future reference. A proper balance between liquid and dry ingredients will produce dough that maintains rise and will support the pizza toppings. It will provide your pizza crust "bite" with tender and moist texture characteristics. To alter the dough recipes increase or decrease the water a tablespoon at a time until you achieve the desired consistency. Soft dough will have higher water content. It will rise quickly when baking, creating a porous crumb structure. If you like a stiff dough and cracker type crust you should lower the moisture content in the dough.

New York style thin crust pizza dough generally has a moisture content of around 55%. The pizza rounds (skins) are usually hand formed. Chicago deep dish pizza dough generally ranges around 60% or more moisture content.

Flour Substitutions and Flavor Enhancers

To alter the flavor of your dough you can experiment with various flours. Select those that marry well with your pizza toppings. Substitute your choice of flour with a portion of the wheat flour. Whole grain flour such as oats and rye can replace up 15–25% of the wheat flour. Most flour substitutions will require a small increase in water and a slightly longer absorption time. To maintain the integrity of your dough limit the weight of the substitutions.

Some flavor enhancers can be added in moderation to the dough. Garlic and onion powder should not exceed 1% of the flour weight, or your dough can relax excessively and become soft and sticky. You can add Parmesan or Pecorino Romano to your flour up to 5–10% of flour weight. You may find this cheese better utilized for topping your pizza just prior to baking or immediately after baking.

Retarding Dough

Retarding dough (storing under refrigeration) makes it possible to prepare the dough in advance for later use. Fermentation continues while the dough is refrigerated but at a much slower rate. A cold refrigerator from 34–36° will prevent your dough rising too quickly while it is retarding. When you retard your dough in the refrigerator for up to 72 hours it will have better flavor, and be softer and easier to form. If you retard it too long the dough can become overly soft and unusable. Similar results can be anticipated if your refrigerator is not cold enough.

To prepare your dough for retarding mix it and place it in a bowl lightly sprayed with oil. Turn the dough over to coat it with the oil and prevent crusting. Cover it with a wet towel or plastic wrap. Allow the dough to ferment for 1½–2 hours at room temperature until it is at least doubled in size. When dough is sufficiently fermented you can poke it with the tip of your finger and the indentation will remain. Punch the dough down when it has sufficiently risen and remove it to your work surface. Scale your dough to the desired weight and form it into dough balls. Lightly spray some oil in bowls large enough to allow the dough balls to triple in size. Press the dough balls down to coat them with oil and then turn them over to prevent crusting. Cover them with lids.

Now that your dough is ready to retard place it in your freezer for 30–45 minutes. This will quickly lower the dough temperature slowing fermentation. Use a timer or you may end up with frozen dough. If you forget about the dough and it freezes you can thaw it in the refrigerator and still use it. After you remove your dough from the freezer place it in your refrigerator and use within 24–72 hours for best results.

Once you remove the retarded dough rounds from refrigeration allow them to rise at normal room temperature for approximately 2 hours until at least doubled in size. Do not allow your dough to rise too long or it will soften excessively, blister, collapse and become unusable. When they are ready to top form the dough balls into rounds and proceed.

Blistering and Bubbling
Some of us pizza lovers like the rustic appearance that bubbling produces while baking. Others may find it objectionable. Allowing your dough sufficient time to ferment prior to baking will lessen extreme blistering and bubbling. Pricking your dough round with a fork or dough docker will also help limit bubbling and reduce their size.

Doughy/Gummy Layer
Doughy/Gummy layer will produce an undesirable surface layer on your dough round. This translucent, grayish, soggy layer is formed while baking. Inferior flour and improper use of toppings can be contributing factors, resulting in uncooked pizza dough.

Beware of allowing a watery sauce to rest too long directly on the bare dough. You can form a flavorful shield between the exposed dough round and the sauce with oil and cheese. Brush your dough rounds surface with garlic herb olive oil and apply a layer of cheese. The cheese layer will also act as a glue to help prevent "pizza slide". Pizza slide occurs when the toppings slide off the pizza crust, perhaps onto your lap or even more embarrassing, your guests.

Raw vegetable toppings and/or shellfish that tend to water off during baking should be used in moderation. Too many can create a swampy pizza preventing your dough baking all the way through. Roasting, grilling or sautéing your vegetables prior to topping your pizza will reduce watering off.

Storage
Flour will not perform well when cold and ideally should be stored in a well ventilated dry space at 70–80°. Flour stored in a very dry climate may require a little more water in the dough recipe than flour stored in a wet humid climate. Flour absorbs odors and should not be stored with onions or garlic, or be in the vicinity of other strong odors.

Commercial Dough Products
One of the most important and fun things about pizza is in the formulation and mixing of the dough. It is essential for an exceptional pizza. For those in the fast lane there are commercial dough products and pizza skins available for purchase. They can shorten the pizza prep process considerably. These products may compromise the quality of the baked pizza. You may find compromise necessary due to your lifestyle. In this case experiment with various products until you find one that best fits your schedule and taste.

Pizza Dough Recipes

Dough Notes:

For Deep Dish Pizza Pie pizza use All Purpose Flour.

Water amounts may vary in recipes by an ounce or more depending on humidity.

It is easier to add additional dry ingredients than it is to add liquid to correct dough mixture.

Basic Dough Recipe

16 ounces Unbleached Bread Flour

2 ounces Corn Muffin Mix or additional Bread Flour

1 teaspoon Garlic Powder/Onion Powder Mix (optional)

1 teaspoon Sea Salt or Salt of choice

2 teaspoons Instant Yeast

10–11 ounces warm Water

1 teaspoon Honey

2 tablespoons Garlic Herb Olive Oil (GHO)

Assemble all Ingredients. Select preferred method to process dough from Processing Pizza Dough and follow instructions.

Poppy Seed Dough Recipe

18 ounces Unbleached Bread Flour

1 tablespoon poppy seeds

1 teaspoon Sea Salt or Salt of choice

2 teaspoons Instant Yeast

10–11 ounces warm Water

1 teaspoon Honey

2 tablespoons Garlic Herb Olive Oil (GHO)

Assemble all Ingredients. Select preferred method to process dough from Processing Pizza Dough and follow instructions.

Whole Wheat Dough Recipe

14 ounces Unbleached Bread Flour

4 ounces Whole Wheat Flour

1 teaspoon Garlic Powder/Onion Powder Mix (optional)

1 teaspoon Sea Salt or Salt of choice

2 teaspoons Instant Yeast

11–12 ounces warm Water

1 tablespoon Honey

2 tablespoons Garlic Herb Olive Oil (GHO)

Assemble all Ingredients. Select preferred method to process dough from Processing Pizza Dough and follow instructions.

Dark Rye Dough Recipe

14 ounces Unbleached Bread Flour

 4 ounces Dark Rye Flour

1 tablespoon Caraway Seeds

1 teaspoon Sea Salt or Salt of choice

2 teaspoons Instant Yeast

11–12 ounces warm Water

1 tablespoon Honey

2 tablespoons Garlic Herb Olive Oil (GHO)

Assemble all Ingredients. Select preferred method to process dough from Processing Pizza Dough and follow instructions.

Masa Harina Dough Recipe

14 ounces Unbleached Bread Flour

4 ounces Masa Harina Flour

1 teaspoon Garlic Powder/Onion Powder Mix (optional)

1 teaspoon Sea Salt or Salt of choice

2 teaspoons Instant Yeast

11–12 ounces warm Water

1 teaspoon Honey

2 tablespoons Garlic Herb Olive Oil (GHO)

Assemble all Ingredients. Select preferred method to process dough from Processing Pizza Dough and follow instructions.

Corn Flour Dough Recipe

14 ounces Unbleached Bread Flour

4 ounces Corn Flour (not Corn Meal)

1 teaspoon Garlic Powder/Onion Powder Mix (optional)

1 teaspoon Sea Salt or Salt of choice

2 teaspoons Instant Yeast

11–12 ounces warm Water

1 teaspoon Honey

2 tablespoons Garlic Herb Olive Oil (GHO)

Assemble all Ingredients. Select preferred method to process dough from Processing Pizza Dough and follow instructions.

Processing Dough by Hand

Mix the dry ingredients including the Instant Dry Yeast together in a large bowl. Form a well in the center of the mixture.

In a separate bowl stir the honey into the water to blend.

1. Pour the water and honey blend into the well. Stir in the flour with a fork to roughly incorporate.

2. Knead the dough in the bowl for 2 minutes. Knead it by pressing down and forward on the dough with the heel of your hand. Turn it slightly and fold it over and repeat. Make an indentation in the center of the dough and add garlic herb oil (GHO) to it. Fold it over and knead it for an additional 1 minute.

3. Transfer the dough to a work surface and knead it approximately 7 minutes more until the desired texture is achieved and the dough is smooth and elastic.

4. The kneaded dough is now ready to ferment.

5. Spray or brush oil into a large bowl and place the dough in it. Press down on the dough and turn it over to coat it with the oil and prevent crusting.

6. Cover the dough with a plastic wrap or wet towel and let it ferment 1½–2½ hours at normal room temperature until it is at least doubled in size.

7. Punch the dough down and remove it to the work surface.

8. Scale the dough into four 7 oz. portions. Form the dough balls by cupping each portion in your hands and rolling it into a dough ball. Fold the dough ball under stretching the outer membrane. Pinch the bottom of the dough ball together between your thumb and forefinger to form a smooth round ball.

9. Spray or brush oil in 4 round bowls large enough to allow the dough balls to triple in size.

Press the dough balls down in the bowls and turn them over to coat with oil. Cover with lids. Refrigerate 24–72 hours. Remove the dough balls from the refrigerator and let them rise until at least doubled in size (approximately 2 hours at normal room temperature). The dough balls are now ready to hand form into 10 inch rounds. Top them, peel them, bake them.

1

2

3

4

5

6

7

8

9

Processing Dough with Upright Mixer

Pour the honey into a bowl with 105–110 degree water and stir to blend. Add the Active Dry Yeast and proof ten minutes to activate. (If you substitute Instant Dry Yeast or Compressed Yeast for the Active Dry Yeast exclude it from the blend and instead add to the dry ingredients.) Incorporate the dry ingredients together in the mixers bowl.

1. Pour the proofed yeast blend into the mixing bowl with the dry ingredients.
2. Stir with a spoon to roughly incorporate.
3. Mix the dough with the dough hook for 2 minutes at low speed (speed 2) and turn the mixer off. Add the garlic herb oil to the dough.
4. Mix the dough an additional 5 minutes. I mix on speed '2' from a choice of 1–10 speeds. If you notice the dough sticking to the bottom of the mixing bowl the dough is too wet. You may need to add additional flour a tablespoon at a time to correct. If you notice the dough is not cleaning the sides of the mixing bowl you may need to add additional water a tablespoon at a time.
5. Remove the dough from the mixing bowl to the work surface. Knead the dough briefly by pressing down and forward on the dough with the heel of your hand. Turn it slightly and fold it over and repeat until the dough is smooth and elastic.
6. Spray or brush oil into a large bowl and place the dough in it. Press down on it and turn it over to coat with oil and prevent crusting.
7. Cover the dough with a plastic wrap or wet towel and let it ferment 1½–2½ hours at normal room temperature until the dough is at least doubled in size.
8. Now the dough has doubled in size and is ready to punch down.
9. Punch the dough down and remove it to the work surface.

Scale the dough into four 7 oz. portions. Form the dough balls by cupping each portion in your hands and rolling it into a dough ball. Fold the dough ball under stretching the outer membrane. Pinch the bottom of the dough ball together between your thumb and forefinger to form a smooth round ball. Spray or brush oil in 4 round bowls large enough to allow the dough balls to triple in size. Press the dough balls down in the bowls and turn them over to coat with oil. Cover with lids.

    Refrigerate dough balls 24–72 hours. Remove them from the refrigerator and let them rise until at least doubled in size (approximately 2 hours at normal room temperature). The dough balls are now ready to hand form into 10 inch rounds. Top them, peel them, bake them!

1

2

3

4

5

6

7

8

9

Processing Dough with Food Processor

If you don't have a large enough food processor that is capable of processing all the ingredients at once you may need to reduce all the recipe ingredients by half.

Pour the honey into a bowl with 105–110 degree water and stir to blend.

Mix the dry ingredients including "Instant Dry Yeast" together into the processors bowl and pulse twice with the metal blade.

1. With the processor running pour the water honey blend through the feed tube into the mixing bowl for 20 seconds and turn off.

2. Remove the processors top and pour garlic herb oil over the dough mix.

3. Replace the top and process the dough approximately 40 seconds until dough forms ball.

4. Remove the dough from the mixing bowl to the work surface.

5. Knead the dough briefly by pressing down and forward on the dough with the heel of the hand. Turn it slightly and fold it over and repeat until the dough is smooth and elastic.

6. Spray or brush oil into a large bowl and place the dough in it. Press down on the dough and turn it over to coat it with the oil and prevent crusting.

7. Cover the dough with a plastic wrap or wet towel and let it ferment 1½–2½ hours until it is at least doubled in size.

8. Punch the dough down and remove it to the work surface.

9. Scale the dough into four 7 oz. portions. Form the dough balls by cupping each portion in your hands and rolling it into a dough ball. Fold the dough ball under stretching the outer membrane. Pinch the bottom of the dough ball together between your thumb and forefinger to form a smooth round ball.

Spray or brush oil in 4 round bowls large enough to allow the dough balls to triple in size.

Press the dough balls down in the bowls and turn them over to coat with oil. Cover with lids.

Refrigerate 24–72 hours. Remove the dough balls from the refrigerator and let them rise until at least doubled in size (approximately 2 hours at normal room temperature). The dough balls are now ready to hand form into 10 inch rounds. Top them, peel them, bake them!

Alternative Method for Processing Dough

1. Mix 7 oz of unbleached bread flour with 7 oz of warm water and ¼ teaspoon of Instant Dry Yeast. Stir the ingredients to roughly blend and cover with a wet towel and let them ferment for 12–24 hours at normal room temperature.
2. After fermenting top off with 3 oz of warm water blended with 1 teaspoon honey and let rest 15–30 minutes.
3. Pour and stir the mixture into a mixing bowl containing 9 oz of unbleached bread flour, 2 oz of corn muffin mix or flour of choice, 1 teaspoon garlic powder/onion powder (optional), 1½ teaspoons Instant Dry Yeast and 1 teaspoon sea salt.
4. Stir ingredients together for 30 seconds to roughly incorporate.
5. Using the upright mixer method mix the dough with the dough hook for 2 minutes at low speed (speed 2) and turn the mixer off. Add the garlic herb oil to the dough.

Mix the dough an additional 5 minutes. I mix on speed '2' from a choice of 1–10 speeds. If the dough is sticking to the bottom of the mixing bowl, it is too wet. You may need to add additional flour a tablespoon at a time to correct. If the dough is not cleaning the sides of the mixing bowl you may need to add additional water a tablespoon at a time.

Remove the dough from the mixing bowl to the work surface. Knead the dough briefly by pressing down and forward on the dough with the heel of your hand. Turn it slightly and fold it over and repeat until the dough is smooth and elastic.

6. Spray oil into a plastic bag at least triple the size of the dough and place the dough in it. Place the dough bag in your freezer for 45–60 minutes to quickly lower the temperature and slow fermentation. Remove the dough from the freezer and refrigerate for 24–72 hours.
7. Remove the dough bag from the refrigerator and let it rise 1½ to 2½ hours until at least doubled in size.
8. Remove the dough from the plastic bag to work surface and scale it into four 7 ounce portions.
9. Form the dough balls by cupping each portion in your hands and rolling it into a dough ball. Fold the dough ball under stretching the outer membrane. Pinch the bottom of the dough ball together between your thumb and forefinger to form a smooth round ball.

Spray or brush oil in 4 round bowls large enough to allow the dough balls to triple in size. Press the dough balls down in the bowls and turn them over to coat with oil. Cover with lids.

Allow the dough balls to rise to at least double in size. The dough balls are now ready to form into 10 inch rounds. Top them, peel them, bake them!

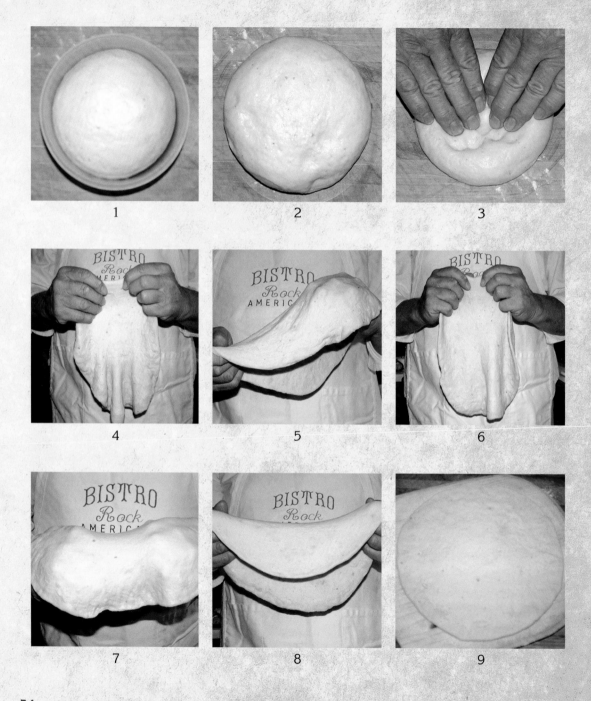

1

2

3

4

5

6

7

8

9

Forming Dough Round by Hand

Cold dough is difficult and nearly impossible to work with. After retarding the dough balls under refrigeration remove them approximately 2 hours prior to use. They should be allowed to warm and rise at normal room temperature until at least doubled in size. If you allow the dough balls to rise too short or too long a time it can make them difficult to work with. Not allowing them sufficient time to rise may result in tearing while forming them. Allowing the dough balls to rise excessively can cause them to over relax and collapse making them difficult or impossible to form into rounds. If experiencing excessive resistance while forming the dough balls into rounds, let the dough relax a few minutes and they will become more pliable.

After forming the dough round place it on a pizza peel spread with corn meal and top it. A perfect dough round is not essential and you may even prefer the more rustic appeal of an uneven dough round.

1. Remove the 7 oz dough ball from the refrigerator and let it rise approximately 2 hours in the bowl with the lid on at normal room temperature until at least doubled in size.
2. Remove the dough ball from the bowl and place it on a lightly floured surface.
3. Pat down the dough ball with the flat of your hand to knock the air out.
4. Pick up the dough round by the edge and rotate the dough one complete turn in a circular rotation. Stretch and pull the dough while leaving a very small rim.
5. Grasp the dough round with both hands and slowly pull and stretch it taking care not to tear it. If there is tearing or small holes develop in the dough simply pinch the dough back together and proceed. Stretch the dough by placing it over the knuckles of one hand and pulling it with the other hand.
6. Rotate and stretch the dough round.
7. Place the dough round over your knuckles and stretch.
8. Grasp the dough round in your hands and pull it stretching it. Work the dough round into a 1 inch diameter. The thickness will be approximately 1/8 inch or less. The dough round will appear almost paper thin in places and will be ready for topping.
9. Spread a pizza peel with cornmeal and place the dough round on it. Make a final adjustment of the dough rounds form.

The dough round is now ready to brush with garlic herb oil. Top it, peel it and bake it!

Once you master this method you can have fun placing the dough round over your knuckles and spinning the pizza into the air with a twist of your wrists. This can help form a nice pizza round.

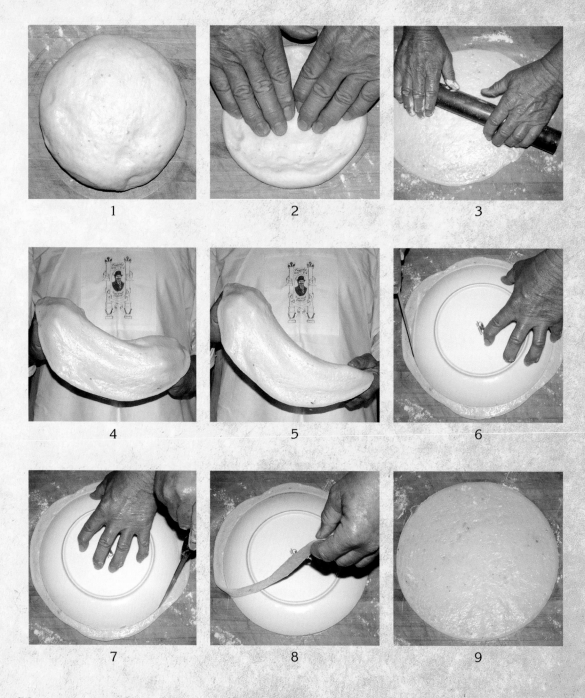

1

2

3

4

5

6

7

8

9

Forming Dough Round with Roller

Cold dough is difficult and nearly impossible to work with. After retarding the dough balls under refrigeration remove them approximately 2 hours prior to use. They should be allowed to warm and rise at normal room temperature until at least doubled in size. If you allow the dough balls to rise too short or too long a time it can make them difficult to work with. Not allowing them sufficient time to rise may result in tearing while forming them. Allowing the dough balls to rise excessively can cause them to over relax and collapse making them difficult or impossible to form into rounds. If experiencing excessive resistance while forming the dough balls into rounds let the dough relax a few minutes and they will become more pliable.

After forming the dough round place it on a pizza peel spread with corn meal and top it. A perfect dough round is not essential and you may even prefer the more rustic appeal of an uneven dough round, eliminating steps 6 through 8.

1. Remove the 7 oz dough ball from the refrigerator and let it rise approximately 2 hours in the bowl with the lid on at normal room temperature until at least doubled in size. Remove the dough ball from the bowl and place it on a lightly floured work surface.

2. Press down on the dough ball with the flat of your hands.

3. Flour the working surface and a rolling pin and roll out the dough into a round exceeding 10 inches. When you roll out the dough turn it over and lightly flour the work surface as often as you need to prevent sticking.

4. Alternate rolling out the dough round by placing it over your knuckles and stretching.

5. Alternate rolling and stretching the dough by grasping it in your hands and pulling it until the desired size is achieved.

6. Place a 10 inch plate over the rolled out dough round.

7. Trim the excess dough with a knife to form a perfect round.

8. Pull the excess dough free of the dough round and remove the plate.

9. Place the dough round on a pizza peel that is spread with cornmeal. The dough round is now ready to brush with garlic herb oil. Top it, peel it and bake it!

Pizza Assembly

Most the thin crust pizzas in this book have an individual weight totaling 19–20 ounces. There is a point at which the weight of the toppings on a pizza can become problematic. With some exception more than 13 ounces of total toppings is not recommended for a 7 ounce 10 inch diameter pizza. You may find fewer toppings with less weight to be preferable. You can adjust the amount, weight and type of the toppings to your preference using substitutions, deletions and additions as desired.

Pizza Assembly is assimilating, blending and balancing the pizza toppings for flavor, texture and presentation. Prior to assembling pizzas preheat the oven to 450° for one hour to heat the pizza stone. Baking time will vary depending on oven type. Experiment until you get it right.

1. Remove the dough ball from the bowl and place it on a lightly floured work surface.

2. Form the dough ball into a 10 inch dough round. (See illustrations of forming dough rounds.)

3. Place the dough round on a wooden pizza peel that is lightly spread with cornmeal.

4. Brush the dough round with a light coating of garlic herb olive oil (GHO) leaving a ½ to ¾ inch rim (yes it is ok to brush the rim also). The oil enhances the flavor and helps prevent "doughy/gummy layer"

5. Spread the Cheese. Cheese placement will affect the composition, appearance and flavor of the pizza. Spreading some cheese directly over the dough round will act as a barrier to "doughy/gummy layer" and help prevent "pizza slide." Pizza slide occurs when the sauce is spread directly over the pizza round and subsequently after baking the toppings slide off the pizza while handling. If you are into living dangerously and not concerned about pizza slide and you want to place all your cheese over the toppings then go for it. Lots of pizza operations do it that way. For those concerned about the pizzas appearance be aware that spreading too much cheese over the toppings may mask them adversely affecting its presentation. Cheese portions and placement can be adjusted to personal taste or eliminated entirely from the pizza. Two possible cheese placement choices.

   Dough round, garlic herb oil, 3 oz cheese, sauce, toppings, 1 oz cheese
   Dough round, garlic herb oil, 2 oz cheese, sauce, toppings, 2 oz cheese

6. Ladle the tomato sauce over the first layer of cheese using a portioning dipper and spread it around with the back of a spoon or utensil of choice.

7. Place the toppings around the inner rim and spread them towards the pizzas center. Place fewer and lighter toppings near the center of the pizza. When baking the pizza toppings will gravitate towards the center of the pizza. Heavier toppings placed near the center of the pizza may result in the pizza slices bending in half while being eaten. This may result in the toppings sliding off, to your pets delight and your dismay.

8. Spread the final layer of cheese over the toppings. You can sprinkle Parmesan or Pecorino Romano over the toppings before or after baking as desired.

Transfer the pizza to the oven and peel it onto the pizza stone.

Bake at 450° F 12–15 minutes until the bread is golden brown and the toppings bubbling. Remove the pizza from the oven and place it on a rack or corrugated surface. Let it rest briefly to maintain crispiness and prevent soggy bottom pizza. Garnish as desired.

Pizza Assembly with BBQ Sauce

1. Brush the dough round with garlic herb oil and place fresh cilantro.
2. Spread 3 oz cheese over the cilantro and drizzle 2 oz of bbq sauce over it.
3. Place 6 shrimp brushed with BBQ sauce over the cheese.
4. Place 1 oz of grilled red and yellow mini pepper strips.
5. Sprinkle ½ oz grilled red onion slices over the toppings.
6. Place 1½ oz each of grilled mango and pineapple tidbits.
7. Sprinkle 1 oz of cheese over the toppings.
8. Peel the pizza onto a pre-heated pizza stone and bake it at 450° F until the cheese is bubbling and the bread golden brown.
9. Remove the pizza from the oven.

Pizza Assembly with Plum Sauce

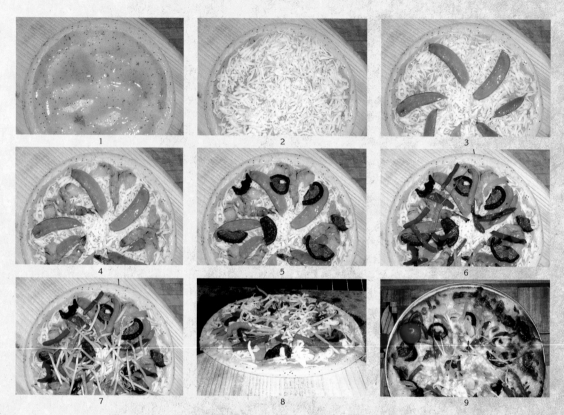

1. Spread 1–2 oz of plum sauce over dough round.
2. Spread 3 oz of cheese over the plum sauce.
3. Place 1½ oz of snow peas over the cheese.
4. Place 6 butterflied shrimp over the toppings.
5. Place 1 oz of shiitake mushrooms.
6. Place 1 oz of grilled red and yellow bell pepper strips.
7. Sprinkle 1 oz of bean sprouts over the toppings.
8. Sprinkle 1 oz of cheese over the toppings and peel the pizza onto a pre-heated pizza stone. Bake at 450° F until the cheese is bubbling and bread golden brown.
9. Garnish the pizza with a cherry pepper.

Pizza Assembly with Salsa

1. Brush the dough round with garlic herb oil and spread with 3 oz of cheese. Ladle 4 oz of Chunky Medium Salsa over the cheese
2. Spread the salsa over the cheese with the back of a spoon.
3. Place 1 oz of grilled polenta strips.
4. Place 2 oz of grilled chicken strips.
5. Sprinkle 1 oz corn/black bean mix over toppings.
6. Place 1 oz of grilled red and yellow mini pepper strips.
7. Sprinkle 1 oz of cheese over the toppings.
8. Peel pizza onto a pre-heated pizza stone and bake at 450° F until the cheese is bubbling and the bread golden brown.
9. Garnish with baby corn and a cherry pepper.

Pizza Assembly with Tomato Sauce

1. Brush the dough round with garlic herb oil and spread with 2½ oz of cheese. Ladle 3 oz of tomato sauce over the cheese.
2. Spread the tomato sauce over the cheese with the back of a spoon.
3. Place 1½ oz broccoli florets.
4. Place 1½ oz sautéed Crimini mushrooms.
5. Place 1 oz red and yellow mini pepper strips and sprinkle 1 oz black olive slices over toppings.
6. Sprinkle 1 oz of cheese and ½ oz fresh grated parmesan over the toppings.
7. Peel the pizza onto a pre-heated pizza stone and bake at 450° F until the cheese is bubbling and bread golden brown.
8. Remove the pizza from the oven.
9. Garnish the pizza with a basil sprig.

Pizza Assembly with White Sauce

1. Brush the dough round with garlic herb oil (spread 1 oz Cheese optional).
2. Place 2 oz of sausage crumbles in a bowl.
3. Add 1½ oz of grilled red and yellow bell pepper strips.
4. Add 1 oz of grilled red onion slices and 1½ oz of sautéed mushrooms.
5. Pour 4 oz of white cheese sauce over the bowls ingredients.
6. Stir the sauce and the ingredients together.
7. Spoon the sauce and ingredients over the dough round and sprinkle ½ oz of Parmesan over the toppings.
8. Peel the pizza onto a pre-heated pizza stone and bake at 450° F until the cheese is bubbling and the bread golden brown.
9. Remove the pizza from oven.

Pizza Pie Assembly

1. Spray or brush oil onto the surface of tart pan.
2. From a 10 oz dough ball form a 13 inch dough round and place in the tart pan. Mold the dough to the bottom and sides of the pan and brush it with olive oil.
3. Place fresh basil sprigs.
4. Cover the basil with 6 oz of mozzarella.
5. Place 9 oz of toppings of choice.
6. Ladle 6 oz of tomato sauce over the cheese.
7. Sprinkle 1oz of Pecorino Romano or Parmesan over the tomato sauce.
8. Cover dough rim with foil and bake 25–40 minutes at 425°. Garnish with a basil sprig.
9. Slice Pizza Pie.

Pizza Peeling Technique & Baking

Pizza Peel—Use it to slide your "topped off" unbaked pizza into the oven onto a pre-heated pizza (baking) stone, and to extract it after baking.

Prepping a Peel—Spread a fine to medium corn meal over your pizza peel to facilitate transference of the pizza onto the pizza stone. Form and place your pizza round on the peel just prior to topping. Immediately after you top your pizza peel it onto the pizza stone. Take care not to let your pizza rest too long on the peel or the pizza may stick to it, preventing it from sliding off.

Peeling the Pizza—Give the peel a little jiggle prior to peeling. Be sure there is pizza movement and the pizza is not sticking to the peel. If the pizza is sticking to the peel try lifting the rim of the pizza where it is sticking and toss some more cornmeal underneath it. After you note proper pizza movement on the peel place your peels tip on the rear of the pizza stone about 2 inches from the edge. Give the peel a slight jerk back sliding the front of the pizza onto the stone. The dough will attach to the stone so you can pull the peel back in a couple short jerking motions, releasing the pizza onto the stone. The first few attempts you may want to experiment with lightly topped pizza rounds to finesse the feel of the peel and perfect your technique.

I like using a wooden pizza peel to transfer the pizza onto the pizza stone and a metal one to extract the pizza off the stone. Either peel can be used for both. Select the peel or peels that work best for you. When you are baking multiple pizzas you may need to occasionally brush the corn meal off the baking stone.

Baking—There are different types of ovens producing a variety of baking results. A convection oven will bake pizza in less time than a standard oven making it impossible to project a standard accurate baking time for all ovens. The amount of toppings you use will also increase or decrease the baking time. You may also want to experiment baking your pizza at different levels in your oven. I used the middle level of mine with good results. You should monitor the pizza carefully while baking until you have established the best approximate baking time for your particular oven. All the baking recipes in this book were developed using a standard oven. The baking time for thin crust pizza was generally around 12 minutes at 450 degrees. The deep dish pizza pie pizza baking time varied from 25–40 minutes. You may need to place aluminum foil around the dough rim of the deep dish pizza pies to prevent burning. Remove the pizza from the oven when the cheese bubbles and the dough turns a golden brown. Remove the deep dish pizza pie from the tart pan and place on a rack or surface that allows air to circulate underneath. Allow it to rest briefly. This will help maintain crispness, preventing steaming the bottom of the pizza and help prevent soggy bottom pizza.

Pizza Toppings—Cheese

Cheese is loved internationally. It is often categorized by the country of origin or degree of hardness. Select cheese that marries well with your choice of toppings and are pleasing to your palate. When baking pizza be aware of the melt, flow, stretch, color and "oiling off"' characteristics of the cheese. Mozzarella and provolone are the favorite cheese toppings for pizza. Other favorites are Asiago, Cheddar, Feta, Fontina, Gouda, Edam, Gorgonzola, Monterey Jack, Montrachet, Parmesan and Pecorino Romano. Using fifty percent mozzarella or provolone will help maintain stretch when blending cheese.

Consumers usually do not have access to manufacturer's cheese specification sheets accessible to stores and pizzerias. They detail moisture, fat, salt, acidity and age, making a comparison of cheese brands possible. It is not necessary for you to have them to select quality cheese. Purchase your cheese from a trusted source that has the flavor and appearance you prefer. Be aware of the expiration date.

Cheese Prep

You can purchase cheese already processed or process it at home. Keep the cheese under refrigeration until ready to prep. Soft cheese is more difficult to process having a tendency to clump up. Placing it in your freezer a short time just prior to processing will make the cheese firmer and easier to shred or slice. Cheese can be sliced, shredded or grated and any blend of these used on pizza. Shredding cheese too small dries it out during baking reducing stretch and causing it to congeal quicker. Larger granules will create better stretch lessening congealing and producing a better appearance. For maximum flavor, hard cheese like Parmesan and Pecorino Romano should be grated fresh just prior to usage.

Cheese Placement

Cheese placement will affect the composition, appearance and flavor of your pizza. Spreading shredded or sliced cheese directly over the dough round will act as a barrier to "doughy/gummy layer." It will help prevent "pizza slide." Pizza slide occurs when the sauce is spread directly over the bare pizza round (skin), resulting in the toppings sliding off the pizza after baking. Too much cheese spread over the toppings will mask them. This may possibly adversely affect the desired presentation. For presentation purposes in this book I used approximately an ounce of cheese to top the pizza. Cheese portions can be adjusted to your personal taste or eliminated entirely from your pizza. Possible cheese placement choices for 10 inch pizzas:

Dough round, garlic herb oil, 3 oz shredded cheese, sauce, toppings, 1 oz shredded cheese
Dough round, garlic herb oil, 2 oz shredded cheese, sauce, toppings, 2 oz shredded cheese
Dough round, garlic herb oil, 3 oz sliced cheese, sauce, toppings, 1 oz shredded cheese
Dough round, garlic herb oil, 2 oz sliced cheese, sauce, toppings, 2 oz shredded cheese

1. Form dough ball into 10 inch round.
2. Brush garlic herb olive oil (GHO) over formed dough round excluding rim.
3. Spread desired portion of cheese over garlic herb oil (GHO).
4. Spread sauce over cheese.
5. Place toppings.
6. Spread final layer of cheese over topping.
7. Sprinkle Parmesan or Pecorino Romano over toppings before or after baking.

Portion the cheese and place where it pleases you. It is your pizza!

Asiago
Asiago is made from cow's milk. It originated in Italy. Flavor changes from mild when young to sharp, nutty and buttery when aged. Asiago's texture changes as it ages from elastic and firm to hard and granular. Traditionally in its whole form young Asiago has a clear or white wax. Medium has a brown wax and aged a black wax.

Cheddar
Prior to 1850 most of the cheese produced in the USA was cheddar. Cheddar is golden or white in color and has a rich, creamy, nutty flavor that becomes more sharp and complex with age. It has been traditional for the color of the exterior wax to denote the flavor or age of the cheese. A clear or yellow exterior indicates mild cheddar with a firm elastic texture. A red wax exterior indicates medium cheddar with a slightly creamier texture than the mild and a fuller cheddar flavor. A black wax exterior indicates sharp cheddar with a texture that is both creamy and crumbly. Cheddar can be flavored with other ingredients. Mild cheddar melts best when shredded and placed under direct heat. Sharp cheddar melts best when shredded and incorporated in a sauce. Cheddar marries well with Monterey Jack for Mexican or Southwestern pizzas.

Feta
Feta is a chalk white cheese with a firm crumbly texture that was originally made in Greece from sheep's or goat's milk. In the USA it is often produced from cow's milk. It has a tart, salty flavor. Feta marries well with tomatoes, oregano, basil, olives, fruit and vegetables.

Fontina

Fontina's country of origin is Italy and it has a brown exterior. It is an excellent baking cheese for pizza with good melting qualities. Italian fontina is ivory to pale gold with a mild, earthy, buttery flavor and supple texture with tiny holes. It has been copied in many countries. The most notable are Denmark and Sweden. Danish and Swedish fontina is pale ivory to light straw color with a slightly tart, tangy, nutty, light earthly flavor. They are mellow to sharp depending on age. Danish fontina has a red wax exterior with rounded corners. Swedish fontina has a red wax exterior with straight corners. Fontina marries well with prosciutto, vegetables, fruit and most pizza toppings. Fontina is similar to Gouda and can be used as a substitute.

Gouda & Edam

Holland brought us Gouda cheese. Gouda is pale yellow and made with whole milk. It has a rich, buttery, nutty, slightly sweet flavor and smooth, creamy texture. A red wax exterior indicates it is mild. A yellow or clear wax exterior indicates it is aged or flavored. A black or brown rind indicates it is smoked. Gouda has good melting qualities and browns at high temperatures. Gouda and Edam are essentially identical in texture, flavor and appearance. The main distinguishing factor between them is that Gouda is always made from whole milk. Edam is always made from partially skimmed milk. Gouda is similar to fontina and can be used as a substitute.

Gorgonzola

This cheese takes it name form the village of Gorgonzola near Milan Italy. Italian Gorgonzola is made from cow's milk and ripens to a soft creamy texture. Its flavor is more earthy than sharp. It is creamy ivory with greenish blue veins and a soft firm and crumbly texture. There are two types of Italian Gorgonzola. Naturale is firmer with a whiter body and has a more assertive flavor. Dulce has a milder flavor and is creamy with yellowish body. It has a full, earthly, piquant flavor and crumbly texture. It adds considerable flavoring in small amounts and is able to withstand high temperatures without burning. Gorgonzola marries well with shellfish, nuts and sweet toppings like caramelized onions and fruits. Gorgonzola is also produced in the USA.

Monterey Jack

Monterey Jack was first produced in Monterey California in the 1890's. It is creamy white with a semi-soft texture. Jack is a high moisture-whole milk cheese that is ripened up to 6 weeks. It has a delicate buttery flavor with good melting qualities. Marry it with mild cheddar for Mexican and South Western pizzas. Another Jack is made from skim milk and aged up to 6 months or more. There are also flavored varieties.

Montrachet

Montrachet is a pure white fresh goat cheese that is soft, creamy, and moist with a subtle tart taste. It comes in a variety of shapes and can be packed in olive oil or coated with crushed peppercorns or edible leaves. It marries well with vegetables, pesto, sun dried tomatoes and Kalamata olives.

Mozzarella

Mozzarella has a delicate mild flavor and blends well with other cheese. Fresh buffalo mozzarella is made in Italy. There is a limited supply available and it can be hard to find in the USA. In the USA the vast majority of fresh mozzarella is made from cow's milk. It is high in moisture and often comes shaped in small balls or logs and vacuum packed. It has a moist, tender, mild, nutty and sweet taste. Always check the expiration date and use as soon as possible after purchase. Discard the mozzarella if it starts to dry out and yellow or if it smells sour. Fresh mozzarella balls can be sliced or diced with a knife or egg slicer. Grating fresh mozzarella is difficult and not advised. It will cause excessive water loss and drying out while baking.

Whole milk and part-skim mozzarella are readily available in the USA. Whole milk mozzarella has richer flavor. Part-skim mozzarella reduces runniness and grease pooling. Mozzarella should bubble and brown lightly during baking and melt evenly. It should not blacken or blister at high temperatures or be overly greasy. Quality mozzarella will stretch and not tear. When melted the texture should be pliant and tender.

Cheese is constantly aging unless frozen. After purchasing keep the mozzarella refrigerated at 34–36° F to slow the aging process and prolong the window of usage. Good quality mozzarella can be kept up to two months. If refrigerated at higher than 40° the aging process will be accelerated.

Underage mozzarella tends to be bland-tasting with a white coloration and a rubbery hard consistency. It bakes poorly, melts poorly and browns with a dry appearance. It will quickly congeal when removed from the oven. The higher the fat and moisture content of the mozzarella the quicker the aging process. During aging whole milk mozzarella will develop a slightly stronger flavor and softer texture with a yellowish appearance. It will have better melting, stretching and browning characteristics. With continued aging the mozzarella's texture changes and it becomes harder to slice or shred. The mozzarella loafs distinct corners will slowly round out and when baking it will tend to oil off and have less stretch.

Mozzarella is best utilized two to four weeks from the date of manufacture. Your store should receive delivery within a couple weeks from the date of manufacture. If you are a food service professional and have access to the manufacturer specifications check the salt and pH level. Select a mozzarella with approximately 1 to 2% salt content. High salt content may cause some blistering, dry spots or small black burnt spots on the surface of the cheese when baked. PH can affect the performance and appearance of the cheese. Too high pH (low acidity) results in brittleness, poor melt and stretch, and may cause excessive blistering. Too low pH (high acidity) can result in mushy texture, poor stretch and inferior flavor. Consult with your distributor and experiment to see what provides you the best results.

Mozzarella can be purchased frozen and processed ready to use. It can be packaged at optimum age by the manufacturer for good baking results when defrosted. Defrost for 24 hours under refrigeration and use within 72 hours. Only defrost what you will use and do not refreeze cheese after thawing. Be aware that defrosted cheese creates surface moisture which promotes mold growth.

Some of this information regarding mozzarella is more relevant for the food service professional. The home pizza maker can easily achieve excellent baking results by purchasing premium processed cheese at your local market or buying mozzarella of your choice and processing (grating or slicing) it just prior to use. You can select from either whole milk or part skim to experiment with. For some variation try blending the two together or with other cheese.

Parmesan

Parmesan is produced in the Italian provinces of Parma, Reggio, Modena, Emilia, Mantavo and Bologna. It is one of the classic hard cheeses of Italy. Parmigiano-Reggiano is the premier Parmesan and its recipe remains unchanged after 800 years. Real Parmesan has its name along with the dairy code and date of production in pin dot writing branded on the wheel. It is straw colored and made from cow's milk. It has a granular texture and sweet, nutty, buttery flavor intensifying with age. It adds a new dimension when grated over pizza before or after baking. The domestic variety must be aged at least 10 months. You can substitute domestic Parmesan if cost is a factor.

Pecorino Romano

Pecorino Romano is another classic Italian hard cheese. It is made from whole sheep's milk. It has a creamy white color and hard grainy texture with a sharp, piquant and nutty flavor. It is aged over one year. Pecorino Romano is more assertive than parmesan and enhances the flavor of other pizza ingredients. It marries well with strongly flavored ingredients such as sausage, prosciutto, pepperoni, olives, onions and bell peppers. It is delicious grated over pizza before or after baking. Domestic Romano is made from cow's milk (in Italian the word Pecora means sheep). Domestic Romano must be aged at least 5 months, has a milder taste and is less expensive than the imported variety.

Provolone

Provolone originated in southern Italy and is also produced in the USA. It is a semi-hard cow's milk cheese with a smooth rind. Provolone has a higher fat content than mozzarella and is sharper and more piquant. When aged the flavor intensifies from slightly piquant when young to sharp. It is aged longer than mozzarella giving the enzymes longer to develop producing a more pronounced flavor. It is often blended with mozzarella on pizza to add more intense flavor. The color changes from ivory to golden yellow as it ages, and the firm texture becomes more granular. Optimally aged provolone is a fine melting cheese. Older provolone is best utilized for grating.

Pizza Toppings—Meat & Chicken

Bacon—Use cooked bacon only. You can purchase it already processed or you may prefer to select your favorite brand and cook it yourself. It can be added to the pizza prior to baking or after.

Canadian Bacon—Is sugar-cured, smoked and cooked. It has low fat content and is much leaner than regular bacon.

Chicken—Use cooked chicken only. Processed chicken is available in a wide variety of shapes and sizes and can be purchased roasted or grilled. You may prefer to grill or roast the chicken yourself and portion as desired.

Chorizo—Is a spicy Spanish sausage that marries well with Mexican pizzas.

Corned Beef—Purchase processed or cook and portion prior to pizza placement.

Ham—Processed ham can be purchased cured, smoked, baked, diced and sliced in many different forms for pizza placement.

Kielbasa—Is a cooked smoked sausage that is highly seasoned with ingredients including garlic. Traditionally kielbasa was made from pork only but it may now be produced with a combination of both lean pork and beef or turkey.

Pepperoni—Is the most popular pizza topping. It is made with beef and pork. The primary spice is cayenne. Two basic types of pepperoni are readily available.

1. American-style pepperoni has orange coloration with a mild to medium spicy flavor. It has a slightly larger diameter than "traditional" and does not cup or char when baking.
2. Traditional or deli style pepperoni has red coloration and is spicier. It has a slightly smaller diameter than "American" pepperoni and is usually sliced thicker resulting in cupping and charring when baked on pizza.

Prosciutto—Is an air-dried cured ham product with a salty/sweet flavor and silken texture similar to ham but more delicate. It is imported from Italy and produced domestically. It is sliced paper thin and can be placed on the pizza either prior to baking, or after to prevent over cooking or burning. Prosciutto is the most popular pizza topping in Italy and France and marries well with asparagus, artichokes, mushrooms, eggplant, peppers, leeks, onions, fruit, Mediterranean olives and goat cheese.

Meatballs —Can be made with beef and/or pork and purchased cooked in various sizes. Purchase small meatballs that are approximately ½ to 1 oz and quarter or slice them for topping pizza.

Salami—Is either all pork or a mixture of pork and beef. Dry cured is sold as "hard salami" and is smaller in diameter than the cooked salami which is softer in texture and milder. There are many varieties blending different ingredients with varying amounts of garlic and spices.

Sausage—Is available in a wide variety of shapes and sizes and can be purchased cooked, sweet or spicy. It is often seasoned with fennel and anise. To avoid grease pooling on the pizza a lean cooked product is desirable for topping pizza.

Steak, Flank or Rib Eye—Buy "choice" grade, marinate if desired, sear on grill and slice at an angle in thin strips. The steak should be "very rare" when placed on pizza to avoid over cooking when the pizza is baked.

Pizza Toppings—Seafood

Anchovies—Strong flavored small fish resembling a sardine. Use Anchovy filets that are imported from Spain, Portugal or France and packed in olive oil. Anchovies marry well with black olives, capers, garlic, lemon, olive oil, shrimp, sausage, tomatoes, eggplant, onions and peppers. After opening refrigerate in airtight containers submerged in olive oil for up to one month or longer.

Clams—You can use canned chopped sea clams in the clam sauce.

Salmon—Purchase salmon filet. The salmon filets should be baked to perfection when the pizza is done. This can be attained by adjusting the thickness of the filet slices. Start by slicing the salmon ¼ inch thick and experiment and adjust as necessary. It is important that the dough and salmon filets are baked to completion simultaneously to avoid the salmon drying out.

Scallops—The two primary scallop types are sea scallops and the smaller bay scallops. Most scallops are shelled and sold in their own liquid. Scallops contain a lot of water. Drain well when prepping for pizza placement. To avoid "swamp pizza" and lessen "watering off," slice sea scallops and use in moderation. Sliced sea scallops were used in this book's recipes.

Squid—Purchase flash frozen and packaged, or have fun cleaning fresh squid and portioning in rings. The timid may want to pass on that. Thaw and blanch squid just prior to pizza placement. To avoid over cooking them and creating a rubbery texture, place the squid on the pizza a few minutes prior to finishing baking, or immediately after baking.

Shrimp—There are four types of shrimp, classified by their shell color. They are brown, white, tiger and pink. Mexican brown shrimp are considered by some restaurateurs as superior in flavor and texture. When the Mexican brown shrimp are unavailable the Mexican white shrimp can substitute. Those taken from the Pacific are preferred by some over those taken from the Gulf. Gulf shrimp are slightly whiter and softer in texture.

Shrimp should be moist with a firm texture and smell like fresh seawater. Because fresh shrimp are perishable they are usually flash frozen shortly after being caught. Beware of shrimp with an ammonia, chlorine, or "rotten egg" odor, and texture that is mushy, chalky, tough or fibrous, and/or are turning pink or have black spots on them.

Shrimp come in a variety of forms and size specifications which designate count per pound. Select a portion size for pizza placement to coordinate with the cooking time for the pizza. If the shrimp are too large they will not be cooked sufficiently. Shrimp that are too small will overcook before the pizza is finished baking. I have had good results with medium shrimp (31/40 ct. per lb.). Butterfly and brush with garlic herb oil and a small amount of lemon juice and marinate for 30 minutes prior to pizza placement. To lessen "watering off" creating "swamp pizza" use shrimp in moderation especially with scallops, fruit or raw vegetables.

Pizza Toppings—Vegetables, Fruit & Nuts

Vegetables and fruits can be used as flavorful and healthful pizza toppings. Include them as toppings to blend, balance and to enhance flavor and presentation. Raw vegetables and fruit can add texture, but should be used in moderation as toppings to minimize "watering off." You can grill, roast or sauté them to intensify their flavor, lessen "watering off" and prevent "swamp pizza."

Select fresh vegetables and refrigerate until use. When prepping, vegetables will start degrading as soon as processed. Return unused vegetables to refrigeration as soon as possible. Avoid using canned vegetables with the exception of canned tomatoes used for making sauce.

To grill, slice the vegetables and fruit to the desired size. Brush the vegetables with garlic herb oil (GHO). Place them on a hot grill and grill until just tender and the grill char lines are pronounced.

Roasting vegetables and fruit is best accomplished with high temperatures in order to caramelize and produce a rich color. Portion fruit and vegetables to your preferred size. Brush vegetables with garlic herb oil and season. Spread single layer on a sheet pan and roast them to your satisfaction uncovered in the oven for 20–45 minutes at 450 F. The high temperature will produce a richer flavor and quicker caramelizing. Closely monitor to avoid burning. Perfectly roasted vegetables are tender inside and slightly charred. Firm vegetables will require a longer roasting time. Roasted vegetables can be stored under refrigeration several days. They will lose their crispiness, but not their flavor.

To sauté, heat sauté pan to a high temperature and add oil to sauté.

GHO = Garlic Herb Oil

Anaheim Chili—Mild green chili that marries well with Mexican and South Western pizza.
Selection: Select firm, smooth and unblemished Anaheim chilies that are 6–7 inches long with an approximate diameter of 1–2 inches.
Preparation: Slice tops off and cut out ribs and seeds, dice or slice into ¼-inch thick slices or strips and brush with garlic herb oil prior to topping.
Storage: Refrigerate.

Artichokes—Artichokes were first introduced to California in the 1880's by Italian immigrants. They marry well with strong flavors like ham, prosciutto, sausage, anchovies, garlic, capers, onions and goat cheese.
Selection: Select marinated artichoke hearts in jars (or purchase fresh and prep).
Preparation: Remove from jar and place on paper towels to remove excess oil. Slice into ¼–½-inch wide wedges.
Storage: Refrigerate after opening.

Asparagus—There is evidence that asparagus has been on the menu since the 3rd century AD. It marries well with ham, prosciutto, sun dried tomatoes, mushrooms, zucchini and goat cheese.
Selection: Check for thin to medium bright green or clear white crispy spears with tightly furled heads. Thin to medium stalks can be used as a pizza topping without blanching or precooking.
Preparation: Rinse and slice off the stalks tough bottoms and discard. Slice into desired lengths and brush with garlic herb oil.
Storage: Prior to prepping refrigerate with stalk's bottoms submerged in water. After prepping keep asparagus refrigerated.

Avocados—Are native to Mexico and Central America and are grown in subtropical or tropical climates, including parts of the USA. They marry especially well with Mexican and South Western pizza, chicken, steak, shrimp, chilies, tomatoes, onions, garlic, cilantro and salads.
Selection: When available select the creamy Hass variety that are black, semi firm and yield to a gentle pressing of the finger tips in a hand grip.
Preparation: Slice in half and remove the seed. Use knife point and slice flesh to desired portion and scoop flesh out with a spoon. To preserve avocadoes spread a little lemon or lime juice over the avocadoes surface and cover with a plastic wrap to prevent discoloration.
Storage: Maintain at room temperature. If purchased green and very firm, you can ripen them by placing them in a paper bag at room temperature. Refrigerate after processing.

Bell Pepper and Mini Peppers—These peppers come in a variety of colors including green, yellow, red, orange and purple. Their color can enhance and add to the visual appeal of the pizzas presentation. They are not hot since they have a gene that eliminates capsaicin which produces the heat in peppers. They marry well with most shellfish, poultry, meat, fruit and vegetables.
Selection: Select shiny and smooth skinned that are firm and without blemishes.

Preparation: Select your choice of pepper and the color and cut you want. Clean and cut the tops off. Remove the ribs and seeds leaving the body intact. Dice or slice into strips or rings and brush with garlic herb oil prior to topping. Peppers can be roasted or grilled prior to pizza placement. Whole peppers can be placed directly over the gas grill on your kitchen stove and charred. Place the charred peppers inside a plastic bag for a couple of minutes and remove from the bag. Scrape off the charred skin and remove the tops, seeds and ribs.
Storage: Refrigerate after prepping.

Bean Sprouts—Often sold as "Chinese Bean Sprouts". They marry well with Asian pizza.
Selection: Select firm unblemished sprouts.
Preparation: Rinse, dry and brush with garlic herb oil.
Storage: Refrigerate.

Broccoli and Broccoflower—Are plants of the cabbage family and are related to cauliflower. They marry well with shellfish, chicken, beef, bell peppers, mushrooms and most other vegetables and sauces.
Selection: Select dark green broccoli with unblemished firm florets.
Preparation: Rinse and slice off the stalk. Slice or break into small florets and brush with garlic herb oil.
Storage: Refrigerate.

Cauliflower—Is related to broccoli and marries well with broccoli, tomatoes, bell peppers and mushrooms.
Selection: Select white cauliflower with unblemished firm florets.
Preparation: Rinse and slice off the stalk. Slice or break into small florets and brush with garlic herb oil. Cauliflower can be blanched prior to pizza placement.
Storage: Refrigerate.

Cherry Peppers—Are also known as Hungarian cherry peppers. They have a slightly sweet flavor and are around 1 to 2 inches round in diameter and become bright red in color.
Selection: Purchase green to red ones found in glass jars at most markets.
Preparation: Use whole for garnish or remove stem and seeds as a pizza topping.
Storage: Refrigerate after opening.

Eggplant—Is native to India and Sri Lanka and found in many countries including the USA and Italy. It marries well with sausage, Kalamata olives, ham, prosciutto, artichokes, mushrooms, peppers, sun dried tomatoes and goat cheese.

Selection: Select male eggplant with a smooth shiny skin and a fresh appearing green stem end. The skin should be unblemished and free of soft brown spots. Male eggplants are preferred because they are less bitter and contain fewer seeds. Female eggplant has a rounder base that is indented at the bottom and looks something like a belly button. The stem spot on a male eggplant is much shallower and may be flat.

Preparation: Steps 3–5 optional. These steps are intended to draw out and rinse off any bitterness in the eggplant. This should not be a problem with most eggplant grown in the USA.

1. Rinse and slice off tops and bottoms.
2. Slice into ¼-inch thick rounds or strips.
3. Place in a colander.
4. Salt the rounds and let rest 30 minutes to draw out the bitterness.
5. Rinse them off quickly and press them between towels to dry.
6. Brush them with garlic herb oil and grill until they are just tender and grill char lines show.
7. For eggplant parmigiana coat the rounds with flour and shake off any excess.
8. Dip them in a mix of half egg and milk and coat with fresh grated Parmesan cheese and Italian seasoned bread crumbs.
9. Fry until they are golden brown and place on paper towels to remove any excess oil.
10. Slice the rounds into wedges or desired portions.

Storage: Refrigerate.

Japanese Eggplant—Is closely related to the potato and tomato. It has more flavor and is smaller than and not as bitter as large eggplant.

Selection: Select those with a smooth shiny skin that have a fresh appearing green stem end. The flesh should be firm, unblemished and free of soft brown spots.

Preparation: Slice off tops and rinse. Slice into ¼-inch rounds or strips and brush with garlic herb oil. Grill until just tender and grill char lines show.

Storage: Refrigerate

Garlic—American white skinned garlic has the strongest flavor. Italian and Mexican garlic are milder and have a purplish skin. Elephant garlic is double the size of the others and much milder in flavor.

Selection: Individual garlic bulbs are generally fresher then those in braids or packages. For fresh or roasting select those that are dry with tight skins and are hard and firm without blemishes. You can substitute diced garlic purchased in jars.

Preparation: Prior to roasting a bulb, remove the loose outer skin and cut off the top portion of the bulb. Drizzle olive oil over the bulb and salt and wrap in foil. Roast 45 minutes or to desired tenderness. After cooling squeeze out paste, or separate cloves and squeeze out individually. Roasted garlic marries well with potatoes, onion and bell peppers.

To prepare individual cloves for roasting, press down on the top of the bulb with the broad side of a large knife and gather the individual cloves with skins into a bunch. Place in foil and drizzle oil over the cloves and salt and seal. Roast the cloves for 45 minutes or to desired tenderness. Set aside and cool before popping cloves from skins.

Storage: Keep garlic in a cool dim place. You can keep roasted garlic refrigerated up to a week.

Jalapeno—Green chili packing fire power. The timid should use in moderation. Use caution when you are handling. Do not touch your eyes after handling without first washing your hands.

Selection: Select dark green chili pods with a cylindrical shape about 2 inches long and 1 inch in diameter.

Preparation: Slice their tops off and remove the seeds and ribs. Dice or slice in rings and brush with garlic herb oil. Sliced jalapeno rings can be purchased in jars.

Storage: Refrigerate.

Leeks—Related to onions but more delicate and mild in taste.

Selection: Select smaller leeks, tender and less woody, with clean blemish-free straight white bases and fresh green tops. Reject leeks with bruised, ragged or dry appearing leaves or bulbs.

Preparation: Cut off upper leaves and rinse bulbs thoroughly under running water. Slice in strips or rings and brush with garlic herb oil.

Storage: Refrigerate.

Mango—A tropical fruit that marries well with other fruit, bell peppers, onion and BBQ sauce.

Selection: Select greenish-red and yellow colored mango that are unblemished, semi firm and yield to a gentle pressing of the finger tips in a hand grip.

Preparation: Rinse off and slice into strips. Place the knife blade under the peel and slice the peel off. Slice the strips into desired portions.

Storage: Maintain at room temperature and refrigerate after prepping.

Mushrooms (Button, Cremini, Portobello, Oyster, Shiitake)—Mushrooms marry
well with meat, shrimp, chicken, olives, vegetables and sauces. Shiitakes have a nutty-earthy taste and marry well with Asian pizza toppings. Their stems are often not used due to their fibrous texture. Portobello have a fleshy beefy flavor and can substitute for meat.

Selection: Some poisonous mushrooms look very similar in appearance to edible ones and can grow in the same habitat. There is no test to determine whether they are poisonous. It is best to leave the harvest of wild mushrooms to the experts and select mushrooms from a safe source. Button mushrooms are white and the most common. Cremini are young Portobello mushrooms similar to Button mushrooms in appearance but darker and more flavorful. They should be smooth, firm and unblemished.

Preparation: Use a soft brush to clean mushrooms or a damp paper towel to wipe off any debris. You can rinse button mushrooms quickly but do not allow to soak. Mushrooms act like a sponge and using water to clean them should be avoided when possible. Slice mushrooms ¼ inch thick. To sauté the mushrooms heat the sauté pan to high. Add garlic herb oil and/or combine it with butter. Add mushrooms and sauté on one side to caramelize and then turn over. Do not crowd mushrooms or they will steam. Properly caramelized mushrooms will have a golden color, tender on the inside and crunchy on the exterior. Sautéing mushrooms will prevent them releasing their water on the pizza while baking. Large Portobello mushrooms can be grilled or roasted and sliced into strips and portioned as desired.

Storage: Keep mushrooms dry and refrigerated. Do not store in plastic bags. They trap moisture and hasten decay.

Nuts (Peanuts, Almonds, Pine Nuts, Walnuts)—Are oily kernels found within a
shell. Peanuts and almond slivers marry well with Asian pizza. Pine nuts marry well with Mediterranean pizza, artichoke hearts, bell peppers, eggplant and tomatoes. Walnuts marry well with prosciutto, asparagus and goat cheese.

Selection: Select premium shelled nuts or use a nutcracker and shell them yourself.

Preparation: You can lightly toast pine nuts in the oven or sauté in a pan. Do not allow them to darken excessively. They will toast more while baking on your pizza.

Storage: Refrigerate after opening to avoid rancidity.

Olives—All olives start out green and eventually turn black as they ripen. They marry well
with Mexican and Mediterranean pizzas, chicken, meat, prosciutto, goat cheese, onions, bell peppers, tomatoes, mushrooms, sun dried tomatoes and pesto sauce.

Selection: Spanish Manzanilla olives are tangy bright green olives that have been lightly lye-cured and are available in a variety of sizes, pitted, whole and stuffed. Cooking can make them mushy and acidic. Add them to pizza after cooking to retain their fresh flavor.

Kalamata olives originate from Greece and are brine-cured. They should have a meaty texture and bit of a bite and can be placed on pizza prior to baking. Due to their stronger flavor and saltiness they should be used in moderation.

Mission olives from California are the best known domestic olive and are a favorite pizza topping.

Preparation: There are five basic methods for curing olives and making them edible: oil, water, brine, dry and lye cured. USA producers commonly use the lye-cured method of soaking the olives in a strong alkaline solution producing mild tasting olives.

Storage: Store with their liquid solution in airtight containers.

Onion—Onions marry well with most anything, unless you do not like them, or they do not like you.

Selection: Premium onions are firm, clean and dry with good shape and should give a dry rustle when shaken. Reject those that are moist or have a bad odor or are sprouting. Small onions produce more waste. Large or jumbo onions are more economical. There are two main types of onions, the sweeter and milder spring and summer onions (also known as early onions) and the more assertive flavored storage onions. The most common storage onions are globe onions and come in brown, yellow and white varieties. White is the mildest. Spring and summer onions have thinner and lighter skins. There a number of well known sweet onions including Vidalia from Georgia and Maui onions from Hawaii.

Preparation: Yellow storage onions are best to use for caramelizing. Sweet onions lose their delicate flavor with long cooking. Red onions can enhance your pizza toppings flavor and appearance. Peel and dice or slice raw onion into strips or ¼-inch thick rings. To grill onions peel and slice onion into ¼—½ inch thick rounds and brush with garlic herb oil, grill and portion as desired. Slice green onions and use as a topping and/or garnishment.

Storage: Refrigerate green onions and store other onions in a well ventilated dry space. Avoid storing onions with potatoes. They will draw moisture from the potatoes and decay quickly.

Pasilla Chilies—Are mild large heart-shaped peppers with thick walls. They marry well with Mexican or BBQ pizza.

Selection: Select unblemished firm dark green chilies.

Preparation: Slice the tops and bottoms off and remove the ribs and seeds. Dice or slice the chili into thin slices or strips and brush with garlic herb oil prior to topping. Whole pasillas can be placed directly over the gas grill on your kitchen stove and charred. Place the charred peppers inside a plastic bag for a couple of minutes and than remove from the bag. Slice the top off, scrape off the charred skin and remove the seeds and ribs.

Storage: Refrigerate.

Pepperoncini—Are a favored pizza topping. The Greek variety is sweeter than and not as hot as the Italian variety. Pepperoncini are flavorful and can add a little heat to pizza. They will marry well with most toppings and can be used as a garnishment. When a recipe calls for cherry peppers you can substitute them with pepperoncini. When prepping peppers you should take care not to touch your eyes.

Selection: Select bright green pepperoncini that can be found in glass jars at your market.

Preparation: Prior to pizza placement, puncture the skin and squeeze excess liquid out. Remove the stem and seeds or leave whole as a garnishment.

Storage: Refrigerate after opening.

Pineapple—Is a tropical fruit that marries well with other fruit, ham, bell peppers, onion and BBQ sauce.

Selection: Use canned or fresh pineapple. Fresh should have a distinct pineapple aroma and light brown yellowish coloration that barely yields to pressure.

Preparation: For fresh pineapple slice off the tops, bottoms, undesirable exterior and hard center. Slice into desired portions. You can roast or grill it to intensify the pineapples flavor and decrease "watering off" when used as a pizza topping. When raw use in moderation to prevent "swamp pizza."

Storage: Refrigerate after prepping.

Potatoes (Yukon Gold)—Have a gold colored smooth skin and buttery flavor.

Selection: Select firm potatoes with smooth unblemished skin.

Preparation: Rinse and slice the potatoes in thin slices. Use immediately or they will quickly degrade. For pizza toppings bake "scalloped potatoes au gratin" (see recipe) and select individual scallops for pizza toppings, or brush potato slices with garlic herb oil and roast or sauté allowing for additional baking time on pizza.

Storage: Store in a cool dry well-ventilated area to prevent them from sprouting. It is important the storage place is not exposed to excessive light in order to prevent the development of solamine. Solamine causes potatoes to turn green and become bitter and indigestible.

Snap Peas—Differ from snow peas in that their pods are round as opposed to flat. Their pod is similar to a normal pea but less fibrous. They are edible when young. The soft and tender pods of snap peas are sweet and succulent.

Selection: Select those with unblemished skin.

Preparation: Wash, rinse and leave whole for pizza placement. Snap pea pods may need

to have the membranous string running along the top of the pod from base to tip removed. They marry well with Asian pizzas.
Storage: Refrigerate.

Snow Peas—Have edible, flat and soft pods with tiny sweet peas and reach a length of 2 to 3 inches. Snow peas are available year round and marry well with Asian pizza, chicken, shrimp, shiitake mushrooms and peppers.
Selection: Select brightly colored, crisp pods that have fresh appearing leaflets and small seeds.
Preparation: Pinch the stems off prior to use.
Storage: Refrigerate.

Sauerkraut—Is a finely-sliced fermented cabbage with distinctive sour flavor.
Selection: Select from the variety offered at your market.
Preparation: Remove from container and drain well prior to pizza placement.
Storage: Refrigerate.

Spinach—Is a highly nutritious leafy green vegetable. It marries well with cheese, eggs, chicken, pork, shellfish, eggplant, onions, mushrooms and tomatoes.
Selection: Select crisp dark leaves without yellow spots.
Preparation: Slice off the stalks and place the spinach in a bowl filled with water to clean. Rinse thoroughly several times and drain dry. Transfer spinach to a colander and firmly press out excess water. To avoid discoloration sauté the spinach in a non reactive pan. Heat the pan and add garlic herb oil, season and sauté until the spinach is reduced. You can substitute frozen defrosted spinach.
Storage: Refrigerate.

Sun Dried Tomatoes—Have an intense tomato flavor. They maintain the nutrients of fresh tomatoes.
Selection: Select premium sun dried tomatoes marinated in oil. They should be bright red, tender and sweet tasting.
Preparation: Remove from jar and drain excess oil on paper towels. Purchase sliced julienne or slice whole ones into strips.
Storage: Refrigerate after opening.

Tomatoes—Are a plant in the nightshade family related to eggplant and potatoes. They are native to the Americas.

Selection: The best indicators of tomatoes quality are their flavor, color, aroma and texture. Fresh vine-ripened tomatoes are delicious but seldom available in most markets. There are available numerous canned tomato products both domestic and imported including whole, diced, chopped, crushed and those combined with purée. Premium tomatoes should be bright red in color and taste fresh, tangy and sweet. They should not taste dull or overly acidic, sour or metallic.

Fresh pack tomatoes are subjected to minimum heat and have a full-bodied fresh tomato flavor. They should be vine-ripened, picked at their peak and canned fresh from the field. Check the ingredients list. There should not be "water" or "concentrate" listed.

Good quality purée should have a bright red color and not a dull red, orange, or brownish color. Tomato purée should feel smooth and creamy in your mouth and not gritty from pulverized seeds.

Select fresh pack ground or crushed tomatoes in a heavy purée. Avoid thin runny sauces that can contribute to doughy/gummy layer and a swampy pizza.

Preparation: When topping pizza with fresh tomatoes they should be used in moderation. Slice thin to avoid excessive "watering off" creating "swamp pizza" while baking. Brush the slices with garlic herb oil. They can also be placed on the pizza after baking. Grape tomatoes can be placed whole on pizza providing visual appeal and flavor without creating "watering off" problems.

Storage: Do not refrigerate fresh tomatoes. Refrigeration destroys a tomatoes flavor and texture. Remove canned tomatoes from cans after opening and refrigerate them in airtight containers.

Yellow Squash and Zucchini—Squash marries well with asparagus, tomatoes, mushrooms, broccoli, bell pepper and goat cheese.

Selection: Select unblemished, firm and shiny zucchini 6 to 8 inches long. Select firm and unblemished yellow squash.

Preparation: Slice into rounds or strips approximately ¼-inch thick and brush with garlic herb oil. Roast or grill to lessen "watering off" on pizza. You can intersperse green and yellow zucchini on pizza for a colorful presentation.

Storage: Refrigerate.

Pizza Toppings—Herbs & Spices

Herbs and spices should provide balance and harmony to accentuate food flavor. They should not overpower or dominate. Fresh herbs and spices have more pronounced flavor. Spices are flavoring ingredients derived from roots, bark, fruits and berries from perennial plants. Herbs are the leaves from annual or perennial shrubs. Dried herbs are best incorporated into the cooking process at formulation. Flavor intensity is increased by crushing them together. Fresh herbs should be placed under the pizza toppings to prevent burning, or placed on the pizza after baking.

The two main herbs used in tomato-based pizza sauces are basil and oregano. They belong to the mint family.

Basil or Sweet Basil—As it is sometimes called has a peppery/mint flavor and is not as strong as oregano.

Black Pepper—Is best when freshly ground from whole peppercorns.

Cilantro—Has a distinct pungent flavor and marries well with Mexican and some Asian pizza.

Oregano—Has a pungent robust flavor and comes in two varieties, Mexican and Mediterranean. Mexican oregano is used in Mexican dishes and sometimes with pizza sauce. Mediterranean includes Italian, Greek and Turkish. Italian oregano is milder than either Greek or Turkish oregano. Oregano is related to marjoram but has a more pungent flavor and aroma.

Parsley—Has a fresh mild flavor and comes in two varieties, curly leaf and flat leaf, also known as Italian parsley. Flat leaf has more flavor than curly leaf and is preferable to use in recipes calling for parsley. Curly leaf is often use as garnishment.

Poppy Seeds—Can be used in dough recipes that marry well with Asian pizza.

Red Pepper—Can be purchased dried in flake form.

Rosemary—Has an assertive aroma and bold flavor with hints of pine and lavender. Its flavor goes a long way and should be used sparingly.

Sea Salt—Is the salt preferred by some food connoisseurs.

Pizza Toppings—Olive Oil & Balsamic Vinegar

The best olive oil comes from cold pressed olives and have a fruity flavor with low acidity. Olives can be pressed numerous times to maximize yields. Olive oil flavors and tenderizes dough and contributes to a golden crust color. The oil's color has relevance to the olive type and origin but no correlation with the flavor. Refrigerate after opening to prevent it from turning rancid. If it clouds or solidifies under refrigeration it will return to its liquid state at room temperature.

Extra Virgin Olive Oil—Is produced from the first pressing only. It has a low acidity level of less than one percent. Extra virgin is used in tomato sauce and brushed over vegetables or drizzled over pizzas. It the sole oil used in the recipes in this book.

Virgin Olive Oil—Is produced from the second and third pressing. It has an acidity level of less than two percent. It has less intense flavor and color than extra virgin olive oil and is less expensive than extra virgin olive oil. It can be used for low temperature frying and sautéing or roasting vegetables.

Pure Olive Oil—Has a light olive flavor and varying degrees of fruitiness, acidity and color. It has a higher burning point and is reliable for cooking.

Balsamic Vinegar—Originates in the Italian provinces of Modena and Reggio Emilia. To be classified "traditional" and receive the DOC seal, balsamic must use grapes from these two provinces. It must be aged a minimum of twelve years. Made the traditional way it tastes like a fine aged port. The flavor is very concentrated and a little goes a long way. The classically produced is expensive and the supply limited.

Most balsamic vinegar from Modena and Reggio Emilia are less costly and belong in another category. In Italy they are called "industriale" and often made by the same producers as "traditional" balsamic, but not subject to the same controls. The better ones are often a blend of high quality wine vinegar, young traditionally made balsamic, reduced must and caramel. They are aged up to 10 years. Balsamic vinegar complements tomatoes and some salad dressings, marinades and sauces. In this book I use it in the tomato sauce recipes or drizzled over Pizza Margherita. Be aware of cheap imitations. The lower quality balsamic tastes like raw vinegar with caramel and herbs.

Sauce & Garlic Herb Oil Recipes

Tomato Sauce

The best indicators of tomatoes quality are their flavor, color, aroma and texture. Fresh vine-ripened tomatoes are delicious, but seldom available in most markets. There are available numerous canned tomato products both domestic and imported including whole, diced, chopped, crushed and those combined with purée. Premium tomatoes should be bright red in color and taste fresh, tangy and sweet. They should not taste dull or overly acidic, sour or metallic.

Fresh pack tomatoes are subjected to minimum heat and have a full-bodied fresh tomato flavor. They should be vine-ripened, picked at their peak and canned fresh from the field. Check the ingredients list. There should not be "water" or "concentrate" listed.

Good quality purée should have a bright red color and not a dull red, orange, or brownish color. Tomato purée should feel smooth and creamy in your mouth and not gritty from pulverized seeds.

Select fresh pack ground or crushed tomatoes in a heavy purée. Avoid thin runny sauces that can contribute to doughy/gummy layer and a swampy pizza.

These tomato sauce recipes will not require pre-heating. They will cook sufficiently while baking your pizza.

The recipes will provide sufficient sauce for four 10 inch pizzas.

Tomato Sauce #1

In a non-reactive bowl combine

16 oz fresh pack crushed tomatoes in a heavy purée
1 tablespoon diced garlic
2 tablespoons extra virgin olive oil
1 tablespoon balsamic vinegar
1 teaspoon dried basil
1 teaspoon dried oregano
½ teaspoon dried parsley
¼ teaspoon salt
¼ teaspoon red pepper flakes
¼ teaspoon fresh ground black pepper

If sauce tastes too acidic a pinch of sugar can be added to reduce acidity. Stir to blend.

Tomato Sauce #2

Place in a food processor 1 oz carrots and 1 oz onion and process.
Transfer to a non-reactive bowl. Add:

16 oz fresh pack crushed tomatoes in a heavy purée
1 tablespoon diced garlic
2 tablespoons extra virgin olive oil
1 tablespoon balsamic vinegar
1 teaspoon dried basil
1 teaspoon dried oregano
1 teaspoon dried parsley
¼ teaspoon salt
¼ teaspoon red pepper flakes
¼ teaspoon fresh ground black pepper

Stir to blend.

Clam Sauce

Add to a non-reactive bowl.

16 oz fresh pack crushed tomatoes in a heavy purée
½ cup drained chopped clams
1 tablespoon diced garlic
2 tablespoons extra virgin olive oil
1 tablespoon clam juice
1 tablespoon balsamic vinegar
1 teaspoon dried basil
1 teaspoon dried oregano
½ teaspoon dried parsley
¼ teaspoon salt
¼ teaspoon red pepper flakes
¼ teaspoon fresh ground black pepper

Stir to blend.

Thai Peanut Sauce

Place all ingredients in a blender and process until blended.

1 cup coconut milk
½ cup Heinz Chili Sauce
½ cup peanut butter
3 tablespoons lemon juice
2 tablespoons oyster sauce
1 tablespoon Sriracha
1 teaspoon sesame oil
1 tablespoon soy sauce
1 teaspoon minced garlic
1 teaspoon ground ginger
2 teaspoons Chinese 5 Spice
¼ cup fresh cilantro
½ cup chopped peanuts
1 teaspoon honey

White Sauce (With Cheese)

Ingredients

3 tablespoons butter

4 oz diced onion

1 teaspoon garlic

2 tablespoons flour

¼ teaspoon salt

16 oz half and half

3 oz shredded Monterey Jack or any good melting cheese of choice

3 oz Fontina, or any good melting cheese of choice

Dice the onion and sauté in the butter until translucent. Stir in the garlic (do not burn). Sprinkle the flour over the onions and stir for several minutes. Add the salt. While stirring pour in the half and half and bring to a simmer. Remove from heat and stir in Mozzarella and Fontina until incorporated.

Pesto Sauce

Combine in a food processor bowl

1/3 cup roasted pine nuts

1 tablespoon diced garlic

2 cups packed fresh basil

½ cup extra virgin olive oil

Process all the ingredients until creamy and smooth. Transfer to a bowl and stir in ¼ cup fresh grated Parmesan.

Garlic Herb Oil (GHO)

Combine all ingredients together in a jar or container of choice.

2 cups extra virgin olive oil

¼ cup diced garlic (use commercially processed diced garlic in a jar)

1 tablespoon dried basil

1 tablespoon dried oregano

1 tablespoon dried parsley

Top the jar and shake to blend. Store refrigerated.

Salsa

Purchase a commercial medium chunky salsa with the heat intensity you prefer. Fresh made salsa is generally too watery and can result in a "swamp pizza" with a doughy/gummy layer.

BBQ Sauce - Enchilada Sauce - Plum Sauce - Teriyaki Sauce

Experiment with different commercial sauces until you find those that work best for you. You may need to thicken your teriyaki and enchilada sauce.

Pizza Toppings Recipes

Black Beans

1 lb. dried black beans

Inspect the beans and pick out any stones. Place the beans in a large pot or bowl and cover with sufficient water to allow plenty of room for the beans to expand. Allow the beans to soak overnight.

Drain and rinse the beans in fresh water. Add to a heated non-reactive pot 2 tablespoons cooking oil and sauté 4 oz diced salt pork until the fat is rendered and the pork crispy. The pork is optional and can be substituted with oil. Add

1 medium diced onion
1 large diced green bell pepper
2 medium diced Anaheim chilies
1 diced jalapeno chili
1 teaspoon dried oregano
1 teaspoon dried cilantro
1 teaspoon cumin
1 teaspoon chili powder
1 bay leaf
1 tablespoon diced garlic (added last to avoid burning)

Add to the pot 6 cups water and the 1 lb beans. Bring to a boil while stirring as needed to prevent burning and then turn the heat off. Transfer the pot to a preheated 425° oven and bake approximately 1½–2 hours. Monitor closely to prevent burning.

Add to the pot 16 oz crushed tomatoes in puree and 1½ teaspoons of salt for the last 15 minutes of baking. Add 1 teaspoon of brown sugar (optional).

Notes:
1. Extract the bay leaf after baking.
2. Adding acidic foods or salt early in the cooking process can toughen the beans.
3. When adding additional water during cooking use boiling water.

Scalloped Potatoes Au Gratin

Coat a 12 by 9 inch baking dish with butter.

3 pounds sliced Yukon Gold potatoes or potatoes of choice
3 tablespoons butter
12 ounces diced onion
1 tablespoon garlic
2 tablespoons flour
1½ teaspoons salt
¼ teaspoon thyme
¼ teaspoon crushed rosemary
3 cups half and half
3 ounces shredded Monterey Jack (or cheese of choice)
3 ounces shredded Fontina (or cheese of choice)
2 ounces grated Pecorino Romano or Parmesan

Slice 3 lbs potatoes and set aside in baking dish. Dice the onion and sauté in butter until translucent. Stir in garlic taking care not to burn. Sprinkle flour over the onions and stir for several minutes to blend. Add salt, thyme and rosemary. Stirring constantly pour in the half and half and bring to a simmer.

Remove from heat and stir in Monterey Jack and Fontina until incorporated. Pour the cheese sauce over the potatoes. Sprinkle Pecorino Romano or Parmesan over the surface. Bake 45 minutes at 425° until bubbling and surface golden brown. Remove from oven and let rest 15 minutes.

Note: Any good melting cheese of your choice can substitute for those in the recipe.

Basic Polenta

4 cups water
1 teaspoon salt
1 cup polenta
2 tablespoons butter

Coat a baking dish with butter. Bring water to a boil in a pot and add salt. Slowly add polenta while stirring. Continue stirring constantly for 20–30 minutes to the desired consistency. Add butter to polenta and stir to blend in. Pour and spoon the polenta into the baking dish and let set. Slice the polenta into grilling portions. Brush with garlic herb oil and grill briefly until grill lines pronounced.

Notes: You can add any number of flavor enhancing foods including half and half or cream, chicken stock, Parmesan cheese or Pecorino Romano, mushrooms and bell pepper.

Hummus

2 cups of cooked chick peas
1 teaspoon diced garlic
4 tablespoons fresh Italian parsley
1 teaspoon cumin
2 tablespoons sesame seeds
½ teaspoon salt
½ teaspoon pepper
3 tablespoons olive oil
1 teaspoon lemon

Add all ingredients to processor mixing bowl and mix. Slowly pour in chicken stock and mix to desired consistency

Thin Crust Pizza

Asian Flavor 82

Caribbean Bounty 90

Country Garden 94

Farmhouse Rustico 115

Paisano Primo 138

Rancho Grande 149

Seafood Harvest 157

Beef - Teriyaki Sauce - Shiitake - Asparagus - Corn - Pepper

Toppings

1. Dough recipe of choice, 7 oz
2. Garlic Herb Oil (GHO), 1 Tbsp
3. Mozzarella Cheese, 3 oz
4. Teriyaki Sauce, 1–2 oz
5. Seared Steak strips brushed with Teriyaki Sauce, 2 oz
6. Asparagus tips, 1½ oz
7. Red/Yellow Bell Pepper strips, 1 oz
8. Baby Corn halved lengthwise, 1 oz
9. Shiitake Mushroom slices, 1 oz
10. Provolone Cheese, 1 oz
11. Cherry Pepper/s garnish

Assembly

1. Form dough into 10 inch round
2. Spread GHO to cover round
3. Spread Mozzarella over round
4. Drizzle Sauce over Cheese
5. Place Steak strips
6. Place Asparagus tips
7. Place Pepper strips
8. Place Corn halves
9. Place Mushroom slices
10. Sprinkle Provolone over toppings

    Bake 12–15 minutes at 450 F until bread golden brown and cheese bubbling.
11. Garnish with Cherry Pepper/s

Chicken - Bean Sprouts - Snap Peas - Shiitake - Bamboo Shoots

Toppings

1. Poppy Seed dough recipe, 7 oz
2. Garlic Herb Oil (GHO), 1 Tbsp
3. Mozzarella Cheese, 3 oz
4. Teriyaki Sauce, 1-2 oz
5. Bean Sprouts, 1 oz
6. Grilled Chicken strips brushed with Teriyaki Sauce, 2 oz
7. Snap Peas, 1 oz
8. Red Bell Pepper strips, 1 oz
9. Shiitake Mushroom slices, 1 oz
10. Bamboo Shoots julienne, ½ oz
11. Carrots julienne, ½ oz
12. Fontina Cheese, 1 oz
13. Cherry Pepper/s garnish

Assembly

1. Form dough into 10 inch round
2. Spread GHO to cover round
3. Spread Mozzarella over GHO
4. Spread Sauce over Mozzarella
5. Spread Sprouts over Sauce
6. Place Chicken strips
7. Place Peas
8. Place Pepper strips
9. Place Mushrooms
10. Place Shoots julienne
11. Place Carrots julienne
12. Sprinkle Fontina over toppings

    Bake 12–15 minutes at 450 F until bread golden brown and cheese bubbling.

13. Garnish with Cherry Pepper/s

Grilled Chicken Stir Fry

Toppings

1. Poppy Seed Dough recipe, 7 oz
2. Garlic Herb Oil (GHO), 1 Tbsp
3. Mozzarella Cheese, 3 oz
4. Teriyaki Sauce, 1-2 oz
5. Grilled Chicken strips brushed with Teriyaki Sauce, 2 oz
6. Broccoli florets, 1 oz
7. Snow Peas, 1 oz
8. Shiitake Mushroom slices, 1 oz
9. Sun Dried Tomatoes julienne, ½ oz
10. Yellow Mini Pepper slices, ½ oz
11. Green/White Asparagus tips, 6
12. Provolone Cheese, 1 oz
13. Cherry Pepper/s garnish

Assembly

1. Form dough into 10 inch round
2. Spread GHO to cover round
3. Spread Mozzarella over GHO
4. Drizzle Sauce over Cheese
5. Place Chicken strips
6. Place Broccoli florets
7. Place Snow Peas
8. Place Mushroom slices
9. Place Tomatoes julienne
10. Place Pepper slices
11. Place Asparagus tips
12. Sprinkle Provolone over toppings

    Bake 12–15 minutes at 450 F until bread golden brown and cheese bubbling.

13. Garnish with Cherry Pepper/s

Pork – Teriyaki Sauce – Shiitake – Mini Pepper – Snow Peas – Broccoli

Toppings

1. Poppy Seed recipe, 7 oz
2. Garlic Herb Oil (GHO), 1 Tbsp
3. Mozzarella Cheese, 3 oz
4. Teriyaki Sauce, 1-2 oz
5. Roasted shredded Pork brushed with Teriyaki Sauce, 2 oz
6. Snow Peas, 1 oz
7. Baby Corn chunks, 1 oz
8. Red Mini Pepper slices, 1 oz
9. Broccoli florets, 1 oz
10. Shiitake Mushroom slices, 1 oz
11. Provolone Cheese, 1 oz
12. Cherry Pepper/s garnish

Assembly

1. Form dough into 10 inch round
2. Spread GHO to cover round
3. Spread Mozzarella over GHO
4. Drizzle Sauce over Cheese
5. Place shredded Pork
6. Place Peas
7. Place Corn chunks
8. Place Pepper slices
9. Place Broccoli florets
10. Place Mushroom slices
11. Sprinkle Provolone over toppings

    Bake 12–15 minutes at 450 F until bread golden brown and cheese bubbling.

12. Garnish with Cherry Pepper/s

Shrimp - Peanut Sauce - Asparagus - Shiitake - Sun Dried Tomatoes

Toppings

1. Poppy Seed dough recipe, 7 oz
2. Peanut Sauce, 2 oz
3. Fresh Mozzarella Cheese, 3 oz
4. Shrimp (31/40 ct. per lb.) butterflied & brushed with GHO & Lemon Juice, 8
5. Asparagus tips, 1½ oz
6. Sun Dried Tomatoes julienne, ½ oz
7. Red/Yellow Mini Pepper slices, 1 oz
8. Shiitake Mushroom slices, 1 oz
9. Peanuts, ½ oz
10. Provolone Cheese, 1 oz
11. Cherry Pepper/s garnish

Assembly

1. Form dough into 10 inch round
2. Spread Sauce over round
3. Spread Mozzarella over Sauce
4. Place Shrimp
5. Place Asparagus tips
6. Place Tomatoes Julienne
7. Place Pepper slices
8. Place Mushroom slices
9. Sprinkle Peanuts over toppings
10. Sprinkle Provolone over toppings

    Bake 12–15 minutes at 450 F until bread golden brown and cheese bubbling.

11. Garnish with Cherry Pepper/s

Shrimp - Peanut Sauce - Broccoli - Shiitake - Mini Pepper - Peanuts

Toppings

1. Poppy seed dough recipe, 7 oz
2. Peanut Sauce, 2 oz
3. Mozzarella Cheese, 3 oz
4. Shrimp (31/40 ct. per lb.) butterflied & brushed with GHO & Lemon Juice, 8
5. Red/Orange Mini Pepper slices, 1 oz
6. Broccoli florets, 1½ oz
7. Shiitake Mushoom slices, 1 oz
8. Fontina Cheese, 1 oz
9. Peanuts, ½ oz
10. Cherry Pepper/s garnish

Assembly

1. Form dough into 10 inch round
2. Spread Sauce over round
3. Spread Mozzarella over Sauce
4. Place Shrimp
5. Place Pepper slices
6. Place Broccoli florets
7. Place Mushroom slices
8. Sprinkle Fontina over toppings
9. Sprinkle Peanuts over toppings

    Bake 12–15 minutes at 450 F until bread golden brown and cheese bubbling.
10. Garnish with Cherry Pepper/s

Shrimp - Plum Sauce - Asparagus - Shiitake - Bell Pepper

Toppings

1. Poppy Seed dough recipe, 7 oz
2. Plum Sauce, 1–2 oz
3. Mozzarella Cheese, 3 oz
4. Shrimp (31/40 ct. per lb.) butterflied, 8
5. Asparagus tips, 1½ oz
6. Grilled Red/Yellow Bell Pepper strips, 1 oz
7. Baby Corn halved lengthwise, 1 oz
8. Shiitake Mushroom slices, 1 oz
9. Fontina Cheese, 1 oz
10. Cherry Pepper/s garnish

Assembly

1. Form dough into 10 inch round
2. Spread Sauce over round
3. Spread Mozzarella over Sauce
4. Place Shrimp, Asparagus tips, Pepper strips, Corn halves and Mushroom slices in bowl and mix with 1 tbsp Plum Sauce. Spread over sauce
5. Sprinkle Fontina over toppings

   Bake 12–15 minutes at 450 F until bread golden brown and cheese bubbling.
6. Garnish with Cherry Pepper/s

Teriyaki Shrimp Stir Fry

Toppings

1. Poppy Seed Dough recipe, 7 oz
2. Garlic Herb Oil (GHO), 1 Tbsp
3. Mozzarella Cheese, 3 oz
4. Teriyaki Sauce, 1–2 oz
5. Shrimp (31/40 ct. per lb.) butterflied and brushed with Teriyaki Sauce, 8
6. Snow Peas, 1 oz
7. Red Bell Pepper thin slices, 1 oz
8. Baby Corn chunks, 1 oz
9. Water Chestnut slices, ½ oz
10. Bamboo Shoots, ½ oz
11. Shiitake Mushroom slices, 1 oz
12. Provolone Cheese, 1 oz
13. Cherry Pepper/s garnish

Assembly

1. Form dough into 10 inch round
2. Spread GHO to cover round
3. Spread Mozzarella over GHO
4. Drizzle Sauce over Cheese
5. Place Shrimp
6. Place Snow Peas
7. Place Pepper slices
8. Place Corn chunks
9. Place Chestnut slices
10. Place Bamboo Shoots
11. Place Mushroom slices
12. Sprinkle Provolone over toppings

    Bake 12–15 minutes at 450 F until bread golden brown and cheese bubbling.
13. Garnish with Cherry Pepper/s

Grilled Jerk Chicken Caribbean

Toppings

1. Dough recipe of choice, 7 oz
2. Garlic Herb Oil (GHO), 1 Tbsp
3. Smoked Mozzarella Cheese, 3 oz
4. Medium Chunky Salsa, 4 oz
5. Grilled Spicy Jerk rubbed Chicken strips, 2 oz
6. Roma Tomato slices, 7
7. Baby Corn chunks, 1 oz
8. Orange Mini Pepper slices, ½ oz
9. Anaheim Chili slices, ½ oz
10. Monterey Jack Cheese, 1 oz
11. Avocado slice/s
12. Cherry Pepper/s garnish

Assembly

1. Form dough into 10 inch round
2. Spread GHO to lightly cover round
3. Spread Mozzarella over GHO
4. Spread Salsa over Cheese
5. Place Chicken strips
6. Place Tomato slices
7. Place Baby Corn Chunks
8. Place Mini Pepper slices
9. Place Chili slices
10. Sprinkle Jack over toppings

    Bake 12–15 minutes at 450 F until bread golden brown and cheese bubbling.

11. Garnish with Avocado slice/s
12. Garnish with Cherry Pepper/s

Ham - Black Beans - Corn - Anaheim Chili - Grape Tomatoes

Toppings

1. Dough recipe of choice, 7 oz
2. Garlic Herb Oil (GHO), 1 Tbsp
3. Smoked Mozzarella Cheese, 3 oz
4. Medium Chunky Salsa, 4 oz
5. Ham slices, 2 oz
6. Black Beans/Corn mix, 1 oz
7. Anaheim Chili slices, ½ oz
8. Red Onion, ½ oz
9. Grape Tomatoes, 9
10. Monterey Jack Cheese, 1 oz
11. Avocado Slice/s
12. Cherry Pepper/s garnish

Assembly

1. Form dough into 10 inch round
2. Spread GHO to lightly cover round
3. Spread Mozzarella over GHO
4. Spread Salsa over Cheese
5. Place Ham slices
6. Sprinkle Bean/Corn mix over toppings
7. Place Chili slices
8. Sprinkle Onion over toppings
9. Place Tomatoes
10. Sprinkle Jack over toppings

    Bake 12–15 minutes at 450 F until bread golden brown and cheese bubbling.

11. Garnish with Avocado slice/s
12. Garnish with Cherry Pepper/s

Mango Pork BBQ

Toppings

1. Dough recipe of choice, 7 oz
2. Garlic Herb Oil (GHO), 1 Tbsp
3. Smoked Mozzarella Cheese, 3 oz
4. BBQ Sauce, 2 oz
5. Shredded roasted Pork brushed with BBQ Sauce, 2 oz
6. Anaheim Chili slices, ½ oz
7. Red Mini Pepper slices, ½ oz
8. Red Onion slices, ½ oz.
9. Grilled Pineapple chunks, 1½ oz.
10. Grilled Mango chunks, 1 oz.
11. Monterey Jack Cheese, 1 oz
12. Cherry Pepper/s garnish

Assembly

1. Form dough into 10 inch round
2. Spread GHO to cover round
3. Spread Mozzarella over GHO
4. Drizzle Sauce over Cheese
5. Place shredded Pork
6. Place Chili slices
7. Place Pepper slices
8. Place Onion slices
9. Place Pineapple chunks
10. Place Mango chunks
11. Sprinkle Monterey Jack over toppings

    Bake 12–15 minutes at 450 F until bread golden brown and cheese bubbling.
12. Garnish with Cherry Pepper/s

Shrimp - BBQ Sauce - Chilies - Peppers - Pineapple - Mango

Toppings

1. Dough recipe of choice, 7 oz
2. Garlic Herb Oil (GHO), 1 Tbsp
3. Cilantro to taste
4. Smoked Mozzarella Cheese, 3 oz
5. BBQ Sauce, 2 oz
6. Shrimp (31/40 ct. per lb.) butterflied and brushed with BBQ Sauce, 8
7. Anaheim Chili slices, ½ oz
8. Red/Yellow Mini Pepper slices, ½ oz
9. Red Onion slices, ½ oz
10. Grilled Mango slices, 1½ oz
11. Grilled Pineapple chunks, 1 oz.
12. Monterey Jack Cheese, 1 oz
13. Cherry Pepper/s garnish

Assembly

1. Form dough into 10 inch round
2. Spread GHO to cover round
3. Sprinkle Cilantro over GHO
4. Spread Mozzarella over GHO
5. Drizzle Sauce over Cheese
6. Place Shrimp
7. Place Chili slices
8. Place Pepper slices
9. Place Onion slices
10. Place Mango strips
11. Place Pineapple chunks
12. Sprinkle Monterey Jack over toppings

    Bake 12–15 minutes at 450 F until bread golden brown and cheese bubbling.
13. Garnish with Cherry Pepper/s

Artisan Vegetable Harvest

Toppings

1. Dough recipe of choice, 7 oz
2. Garlic Herb Oil (GHO), 1 Tbsp
3. Fresh Mozzarella Cheese, 2½ oz
4. Tomato Sauce, 3 oz
5. Red Bell Pepper slices, 1½ oz
6. Grilled Yellow Squash slices, 1½ oz
7. Broccoli florets, 1½ oz
8. Sautéed Button Mushroom slices, 1 oz
9. Pitted Kalamata Olives, 9
10. Fontina Cheese, 1 oz
11. Parmesan Cheese, ½ oz
12. Basil Sprig garnish

Assembly

1. Form dough into 10 inch round
2. Spread GHO to cover round
3. Spread Mozzarella over GHO
4. Spread Sauce over Cheese
5. Place Pepper slices
6. Place Squash slices
7. Place Broccoli florets
8. Place Mushroom slices
9. Place Olives
10. Sprinkle Fontina over toppings
11. Sprinkle Parmesan over toppings

    Bake 12–15 minutes at 450 F until bread golden brown and cheese bubbling.
12. Place Basil Sprig

Artichokes - Grilled Zucchini - Tomatoes - Mushrooms - Olives

Toppings

1. Dough recipe of choice, 7 oz
2. Garlic Herb Oil (GHO), 1 Tbsp
3. Fresh Mozzarella Cheese, 2½ oz
4. Tomato Sauce, 3 oz.
5. Marinated Artichoke Heart wedges, 1½ oz
6. Grilled Zucchini strips, 1½ oz
7. Sautéed Mushroom slices, 1 oz
8. Grape Tomatoes, 9
9. Black Olive slices, 1 oz
10. Fontina Cheese, 1 oz
11. Parmesan Cheese, ½ oz
12. Basil Sprig garnish
13. Cherry Pepper/s garnish

Assembly

1. Form dough into 10 inch round
2. Spread GHO to cover round
3. Spread Mozzarella over GHO
4. Spread Sauce over Cheese
5. Place Artichoke wedges
6. Place Zucchini strips
7. Place Mushroom slices
8. Place Tomatoes
9. Sprinkle Olive slices over toppings
10. Sprinkle Fontina over top
11. Sprinkle Parmesan over top

    Bake 12–15 minutes at 450 F until bread golden brown and cheese bubbling.

12. Garnish with Basil Sprig
13. Garnish with Cherry Pepper/s

Artichoke Hearts - Broccoli - Tomatoes - Mini Peppers - Olives

Toppings

1. Dough recipe of choice, 7 oz
2. Garlic Herb Oil (GHO), 1 Tbsp
3. Fresh Mozzarella Cheese, 3 oz
4. Tomato Sauce, 3 oz
5. Marinated Artichoke Heartwedges, 1½ oz
6. Broccoli florets, 1½ oz
7. Grilled Yellow Mini Pepper slices, 1 oz
8. Grape Tomatoes, 7
9. Pitted Kalamata Olives, 9
10. Fontina Cheese, 1 oz
11. Basil Sprig garnish

Assembly

1. Form dough into 10 inch round
2. Spread GHO to cover round
3. Spread Mozzarella over GHO
4. Spread Sauce over Cheese
5. Place Artichoke wedges
6. Place Broccoli florets
7. Place Pepper slices
8. Place Tomatoes
9. Place Olives
10. Sprinkle Fontina over toppings

    Bake 12–15 minutes at 450 F until bread golden brown and cheese bubbling.

11. Garnish with Basil Sprig

Artichoke Hearts - Pesto Sauce - Mushrooms - Tomatoes - Squash

Toppings

1. Dough recipe of choice, 7 oz
2. Pesto Sauce, 1–2 oz
3. Fresh Mozzarella Cheese, 2½ oz
4. Marinated Artichoke Heart wedges, 1½ oz
5. Grilled Yellow Squash slices, 1½ oz
6. Sautéed Button Mushroom slices, 1½ oz
7. Grape Tomatoes, 9
8. Fontina Cheese, 1 oz
9. Parmesan Cheese, ½ oz
10. Basil Sprig garnish

Assembly

1. Form dough into 10 inch round
2. Spread Pesto to cover round
3. Spread Mozzarella over Pesto
4. Place Artichoke wedges
5. Place Squash slices
6. Place Mushroom slices
7. Place Tomatoes
8. Sprinkle Fontina over toppings
9. Sprinkle Parmesan over toppings

   Bake 12–15 minutes at 450 F until bread golden brown and cheese bubbling.
10. Garnish with Basil Sprig

Artichoke - Tomato Sauce - Red Corn - Mushrooms - Beans - Tomato

Toppings

1. Dough recipe of choice, 7 oz
2. Garlic Herb Oil (GHO), 1 Tbsp
3. Mozzarella Cheese, 3 oz
4. Tomato Sauce, 3 oz
5. Red/Yellow Tomato slices, 1½ oz
6. Marinated Artichoke Heart wedges, 1½ oz
7. Green Beans, 1 oz
8. Sautéed Button Mushroom slices, 1 oz
9. Fresh Red Corn kernels, 1 oz
10. Fontina Cheese, 1 oz
11. Basil Sprig garnish

Assembly

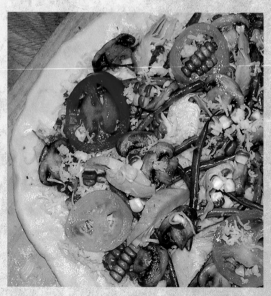

1. Form dough into 10 inch round
2. Spread GHO to cover round
3. Spread Mozzarella over GHO
4. Spread Sauce over Cheese
5. Place Tomato slices
6. Place Artichoke wedges
7. Place Beans
8. Place Mushroom slices
9. Sprinkle Corn kernels over toppings
10. Sprinkle Fontina over toppings

    Bake 12–15 minutes at 450 F until bread golden brown and cheese bubbling.

11. Garnish with Basil Sprig

Asparagus - Artichoke - Broccoli - Bell Pepper - Olive

Toppings

1. Dough recipe of choice, 7 oz.
2. Garlic Herb Oil (GHO), 1 Tbsp
3. Fresh Mozzarella Cheese, 3½ oz
4. Tomato Sauce, 3 oz
5. Asparagus tips, 1½ oz
6. Marinated Artichoke Heart quarters, 1½ oz
7. Broccoli florets, 1 oz
8. Fire Charred Red Bell Pepper strips, 1 oz
9. Pitted Kalamata Olives, 9
10. Pecorino Romano Cheese, ½ oz
11. Cherry Pepper/s garnish

Assembly

1. Form dough into 10 inch round
2. Spread GHO to cover round
3. Spread Mozzarella over GHO
4. Spread Sauce over Cheese
5. Place Asparagus tips
6. Place Artichoke quarters
7. Place Broccoli florets
8. Place Pepper strips
9. Place Olives
10. Sprinkle Pecorino over toppings

    Bake 12–15 minutes at 450 F until bread golden brown and cheese bubbling.
11. Garnish with Cherry Pepper/s

Asparagus - Fresh Mozzarella - Roma Tomatoes - Parmesan

Toppings

1. Dough recipe of choice, 7 oz
2. Garlic Herb Oil (GHO), 1 Tbsp
3. Fresh Mozzarella Cheese, 4 oz
4. Asparagus tips, 3 oz
5. Roma Tomato thin slices to cover round
6. Parmesan Cheese, ½ oz
7. Garlic Herb Oil (GHO), 1 Tbsp
8. Balsamic Vinegar, 1 Tbsp
9. Basil Sprig/s garnish

Assembly

1. Form dough into 10 inch round
2. Spread GHO to cover dough
3. Spread Mozzarella over GHO
4. Place Asparagus tips
5. Place Tomato slices to cover round
6. Sprinkle Parmesan over toppings

   Bake 12–15 minutes at 450 F until bread golden brown and cheese bubbling.

7. Drizzle GHO over Tomatoes
8. Drizzle Vinegar over toppings
9. Garnish with Basil Sprig/s

Asparagus - Spinach - Grape Tomatoes - Mushrooms

Toppings

1. Dough recipe of choice, 7 oz.
2. Garlic Herb Oil (GHO), 1 Tbsp
3. Fresh Mozzarella Cheese, 3 oz
4. Tomato Sauce, 3 oz
5. Sautéed Spinach, 1½ oz
6. White Asparagus tips, 1½ oz
7. Sautéed Button Mushroom slices, 1 oz
8. Grape Tomatoes, 9
9. Black Olive slices, 1 oz
10. Fontina Cheese, 1 oz
11. Basil Sprig garnish

Assembly

1. Form dough into 10 inch round
2. Spread GHO to cover round
3. Spread Mozzarella over GHO
4. Spread Sauce over Cheese
5. Spread Spinach over Sauce
6. Place Asparagus tips
7. Place Mushroom slices
8. Place Tomatoes
9. Sprinkle Olive slices over toppings
10. Sprinkle Fontina over toppings

    Bake 12–15 minutes at 450 F until bread golden brown and cheese bubbling.

11. Garnish with Basil Sprig

Broccoli - Button Mushrooms - Asparagus - Grape Tomatoes

Toppings

1. Dough recipe of choice, 7 oz
2. Garlic Herb Oil (GHO), 1 Tbsp
3. Fresh Mozzarella Cheese, 3 oz
4. Tomato Sauce, 3 oz
5. Broccoli florets, 1½ oz
6. Asparagus tips, 1½ oz
7. Sautéed Button Mushroom slices, 1 oz
8. Yellow Mini Pepper slices, 1 oz
9. Grape Tomatoes, 9
10. Fontina Cheese, 1 oz
11. Basil Sprig garnish

Assembly

1. Form dough into 10 inch round
2. Spread GHO to cover round
3. Spread Mozzarella over GHO
4. Spread Sauce over Cheese
5. Place Broccoli florets
6. Place Asparagus tips
7. Place Mushroom slices
8. Place Pepper slices
9. Place Tomatoes
10. Sprinkle Fontina over toppings

    Bake 12–15 minutes at 450 F until bread golden brown and cheese bubbling.

11. Garnish with Basil Sprig

Broccoli - White Sauce - Sautéed Mushroom - Yellow Squash

Toppings

1. Dough recipe of choice, 7 oz
2. Garlic Herb Oil (GHO), 1 Tbsp
3. White Sauce (see recipe), 4 oz
4. Broccoli florets, 1½ oz
5. Sautéed Button/Crimini Mushroom slices, 1½ oz
6. Grilled Yellow Squash slices, 1½ oz
7. Grilled Red/Yellow Mini Pepper strips, 1½ oz
8. Parmesan Cheese, ½ oz

Assembly

1. Form dough into 10 inch round
2. Spread GHO to cover round
3. Mix vegetables in bowl with White Sauce and spread over Cheese.
4. Sprinkle Parmesan over toppings

   Bake 12–15 minutes at 450 F until bread golden brown and cheese bubbling.

Eggplant - Spinach - Grape Tomatoes - Yellow Zucchini - Olives

Toppings

1. Dough recipe of choice, 7 oz.
2. Garlic Herb Oil (GHO), 1 Tbsp
3. Fresh Mozzarella Cheese, 2½ oz
4. Goat Cheese, ½ oz
5. Tomato Sauce, 3 oz
6. Sautéed Spinach, 1½ oz
7. Grilled Eggplant wedges, 1½ oz
8. Grilled Yellow Zucchini slices, 1½ oz
9. Grape Tomatoes, 9
10. Pitted Kalamata Olives, 9
11. Fontina Cheese, 1 oz
12. Basil sprig garnish

Assembly

1. Form dough into 10 inch round
2. Spread GHO to cover round
3. Spread Mozzarella over GHO
4. Fork Goat Cheese over Mozzarella
5. Spread Sauce over Cheese
6. Spread Spinach over Sauce
7. Place Eggplant wedges
8. Place Zucchini slices
9. Place Tomatoes
10. Place Olives
11. Sprinkle Fontina over toppings

    Bake 12–15 minutes at 450 F until bread golden brown and cheese bubbling
12. Garnish with Basil Sprig

Cauliflower - Tomatoes - Broccoli - Yellow Squash

Toppings

1. Dough recipe of choice, 7 oz
2. Garlic Herb Oil (GHO), 1 Tbsp
3. Fresh Mozzarella Cheese, 2½ oz
4. Tomato Sauce, 3 oz
5. Green/White Cauliflower florets, 1½ oz
6. Broccoli florets, 1½ oz
7. Grilled Yellow Squash slices, 1½ oz
8. Grape Tomatoes, 9
9. Fontina Cheese, 1 oz
10. Pecorino Romano Cheese, ½ oz
11. Basil Sprig garnish

Assembly

1. Form dough into 10 inch round
2. Spread GHO to cover round
3. Spread Mozzarella over GHO
4. Spread Sauce over Cheese
5. Place Cauliflower florets
6. Place Broccoli florets
7. Place Squash slices
8. Place Tomatoes
9. Sprinkle Fontina over toppings
10. Sprinkle Pecorino over toppings

    Bake 12–15 minutes at 450 F until bread golden brown and cheese bubbling.

11. Garnish with Basil Sprig

Corn - Grilled Mini Pepper - Asparagus - Grilled Zucchini - Shiitake

Toppings

1. Dough recipe of choice, 7 oz
2. Garlic Herb Oil (GHO), 1 Tbsp
3. Fresh Mozzarella Cheese, 2½ oz
4. Tomato Sauce, 3 oz
5. Grilled Red/Yellow Mini Pepper strips, 1½ oz
6. Asparagus tips, 1½ oz
7. Grilled Zucchini strips, 1 oz
8. Shiitake Mushrooms slices, 1 oz
9. Fresh Corn kernels, 1 oz
10. Fontina Cheese, 1 oz
11. Parmesan Cheese, ½ oz
12. Basil Sprig garnish

Assembly

1. Form dough into 10 inch round
2. Spread GHO to cover round
3. Spread Mozzarella over GHO
4. Spread Sauce over Cheese
5. Place Pepper strips
6. Place Asparagus tips
7. Place Zucchini strips
8. Place Mushroom slices
9. Sprinkle Corn over toppings
10. Sprinkle Fontina over toppings
11. Sprinkle Parmesan over toppings
    Bake 12–15 minutes at 450 F until bread golden brown and cheese bubbling.
12. Garnish with Basil Sprig

Japanese Eggplant - Tomatoes - Artichoke Hearts - Mushrooms

Toppings

1. Dough recipe of choice, 7 oz
2. Garlic Herb Oil (GHO), 1 Tbsp
3. Fresh Mozzarella Cheese, 3 oz
4. Tomato Sauce, 3 oz
5. Marinated Artichoke Heart wedges, 1½ oz
6. Grilled Japanese Eggplant slices,1½ oz
7. Sautéed Crimini Mushroom slices, 1 oz
8. Marinated Sun Dried Tomatoes julienne, ½ oz
9. Yellow Mini Pepper slices, ½ oz
10. Pitted Kalamata Olives, 9
11. Fontina Cheese, 1 oz
12. Basil sprig

Assembly

1. Form dough into 10 inch round
2. Spread GHO to cover round
3. Spread Mozzarella over GHO
4. Spread Sauce over Cheese
5. Place Artichoke wedges
6. Place Eggplant slices
7. Place Mushroom slices
8. Place Tomatoes julienne
9. Place Pepper slices
10. Place Olives
11. Sprinkle Fontina over toppings

    Bake 12–15 minutes at 450 F until bread golden brown and cheese bubbling.
12. Garnish with Basil sprig

Japanese Eggplant - Tomatoes - Asparagus - Mini Pepper - Olive

Toppings

1. Dough recipe of choice, 7 oz.
2. Garlic Herb Oil (GHO), 1 Tbsp
3. Fresh Mozzarella Cheese, 2½ oz
4. Tomato Sauce, 3 oz
5. Asparagus tips, 1½ oz
6. Grilled Japanese Eggplant slices, 1½ oz
7. Yellow Mini Pepper slices, 1 oz
8. Grape Tomatoes, 9
9. Pitted Kalamata Olives, 9
10. Fontina Cheese, 1 oz
11. Parmesan Cheese, ½ oz
12. Pepperoncini garnish
13. Basil Sprig garnish

Assembly

1. Form dough into 10 inch round
2. Spread GHO to cover round
3. Spread Mozzarella over GHO
4. Spread Sauce over Cheese
5. Place Asparagus tips
6. Place Eggplant slices
7. Place Pepper slices
8. Place Tomatoes
9. Place Olives
10. Sprinkle Fontina over toppings
11. Sprinkle Parmesan over toppings
    Bake 12–15 minutes at 450 F until bread golden brown and cheese bubbling.
12. Garnish with Pepperoncini
13. Garnish with Basil Sprig

Mushrooms - Hummus - Japanese Eggplant - Grape Tomatoes

Toppings

1. Dough recipe of choice, 7 oz
2. Hummus, 3 oz
3. Mozzarella Cheese, 3 oz
4. Broccoflower florets, 1½ oz
5. Grilled Japanese Eggplant slices, 1½ oz
6. Shiitake/Oyster Mushroom slices, 1 oz
7. Grape Tomatoes, 9
8. Roasted Garlic cloves, ½ oz
9. Pitted Kalamata Olives, 9
10. Fontina Cheese, 1 oz
11. Cherry Pepper/s garnish

Assembly

1. Form dough into 10 inch round
2. Spread Hummus over dough round
3. Spread Mozzarella over Hummus
4. Place Broccoflower florets
5. Place Eggplant slices
6. Place Mushroom slices
7. Place Tomatoes
8. Place Garlic cloves
9. Place Olives
10. Sprinkle Fontina over toppings

    Bake 12–15 minutes at 450 F until bread golden brown and cheese bubbling.

11. Garnish with Cherry Pepper/s

Rainbow Vegetable

Toppings

1. Dough recipe of choice, 7 oz.
2. Garlic Herb Oil (GHO), 1 Tbsp
3. Fresh Mozzarella Cheese, 2½ oz
4. Tomato Sauce, 3 oz
5. Grilled Zucchini strips, 2 oz
6. Grilled red Bell Pepper strips, 2 oz
7. Asparagus tips, 2 oz
8. Fontina Cheese, 1 oz
9. Parmesan Cheese, ½ oz
10. Basil Sprig garnish

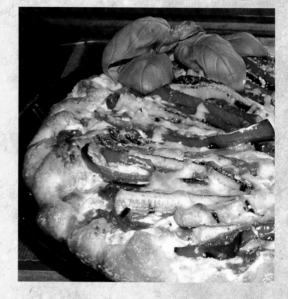

Assembly

1. Form dough into 10 inch round
2. Spread GHO to cover round
3. Spread Mozzarella over GHO
4. Spread Sauce over Cheese
5. Place Zucchini slices
6. Place Pepper slices
7. Place Asparagus strips
8. Sprinkle Fontina over toppings
9. Sprinkle Parmesan over toppings

    Bake 12–15 minutes at 450 F until bread golden brown and cheese bubbling.

10. Garnish with Basil Sprig

Sautéed Mushroom - Broccoli - Kalamata Olive - Bell Pepper

Toppings

1. Dough recipe of choice, 7 oz
2. Garlic Herb Oil (GHO), 1 Tbsp
3. Fresh Mozzarella Cheese, 2½ oz
4. Tomato Sauce, 3 oz
5. Red Bell Pepper slices, 1½ oz
6. Broccoli florets, 1½ oz
7. Sautéed Button Mushroom slices, 1½ oz
8. Pitted Kalamata Olives, 9
9. Fontina Cheese, 1 oz
10. Parmesan Cheese, ½ oz
11. Basil Sprig garnish

Assembly

1. Form dough into 10 inch round
2. Spread GHO to cover round
3. Spread Mozzarella over GHO
4. Spread Sauce over Cheese
5. Place Pepper slices
6. Place Broccoli florets
7. Place Mushroom slices
8. Place Olives
9. Sprinkle Fontina over toppings
10. Sprinkle Parmesan over toppings

    Bake 12–15 minutes at 450 F until bread golden brown and cheese bubbling.

11. Place Basil Sprig

Spinach – Mushroom – Pepper – Corn – Tomatoes – Onion – Olive

Toppings

1. Dough recipe of choice, 7 oz
2. Garlic Herb Oil (GHO), 1 Tbsp
3. Fresh Mozzarella Cheese, 3 oz
4. Tomato Sauce, 3 oz
5. Spinach sautéed, 1½ oz
6. Sautéed Crimini Mushroom slices, 1 oz
7. Corn Kernels, ½ oz
8. Red Onion slices, ½ oz
9. Orange Mini Pepper slices, ½ oz
10. Grape Tomatoes, 9
11. Pitted Kalamata Olives, 9
12. Provolone Cheese, 1 oz
13. Basil Sprig garnish
14. Baby Corn garnish

Assembly

1. Form dough into 10 inch round
2. Spread GHO to cover round
3. Spread Mozzarella over GHO
4. Spread Sauce over Cheese
5. Spread Spinach slices
6. Place Mushroom slices
7. Sprinkle Corn over toppings
8. Place Onion slices
9. Place Pepper slices
10. Place Tomatoes
11. Place Olives
12. Sprinkle Provolone over toppings

    Bake 12–15 minutes at 450 F until bread golden brown and cheese bubbling.

13. Garnish with Cherry Pepper/s and Baby Corn

Tomatoes - Artichoke Hearts - Asparagus - Yellow Zucchini

Toppings

1. Dough recipe of choice, 7 oz.
2. Garlic Herb Oil (GHO), 1 Tbsp
3. Fresh Mozzarella Cheese, 3 oz
4. Tomato Sauce, 3 oz
5. Asparagus tips, 1½ oz
6. Grilled Yellow Zucchini strips, 1½ oz
7. Marinated Artichoke Heart wedges, 1 oz
8. Grape Tomatoes, 9
9. Pitted Kalamata Olives, 9
10. Fontina Cheese, 1 oz
11. Basil Sprig garnish

Assembly

1. Form dough into 10 inch round
2. Spread GHO to cover round
3. Spread Mozzarella over GHO
4. Spread Sauce over Cheese
5. Place Asparagus tips
6. Place Zucchini strips
7. Place Artichoke wedges
8. Place Tomatoes
9. Place Olives
10. Sprinkle Fontina over toppings

    Bake 12–15 minutes at 450 F until bread golden brown and cheese bubbling.

11. Garnish with Basil Sprig

Yellow Squash – Potatoes au Gratin – Zucchini – Mushrooms – Pepper

Toppings

1. Dough recipe of choice, 7 oz
2. Garlic Herb Oil (GHO), 1 Tbsp
3. Fresh Mozzarella Cheese, 2½ oz
4. Tomato Sauce, 3 oz
5. Potatoes au Gratin slices, 2 oz
6. Yellow Squash slices, 1 oz
7. Zucchini slices, 1 oz
8. Red Mini Pepper slices, ½ oz
9. Sautéed Mushroom slices, 1 oz
10. Red Onion slices, ½ oz
11. Fontina Cheese, 1 oz
12. Parmesan Cheese, ½ oz
13. Cherry Pepper/s garnish

Assembly

1. Form dough into 10 inch round
2. Spread GHO to cover round
3. Spread Mozzarella over GHO
4. Spread Sauce over Cheese
5. Place Potato slices
6. Place Squash slices
7. Place Zucchini slices
8. Place Pepper slices
9. Place Mushroom slices
10. Sprinkle Onion over toppings
11. Sprinkle Fontina over toppings
12. Sprinkle Parmesan over toppings

    Bake 12–15 minutes at 450 F until bread golden brown and cheese bubbling.

13. Garnish with Cherry Peppers

Black Forest Ham - Kielbasa - Sausage - Tomato Sauce - Olive

Toppings

1. Dough recipe of choice, 7 oz
2. Garlic Herb Oil (GHO), 1 Tbsp
3. Mozzarella Cheese, 3 oz
4. Tomato Sauce, 3 oz
5. Black Forest Ham slices, 1½ oz
6. Grilled Kielbasa slices, 1½ oz
7. Sausage crumbles, 1 oz
8. Red/Yellow Mini Pepper slices, 1 oz
9. Black Olive slices, 1 oz
10. Provolone Cheese, 1 oz.
11. Cherry Pepper/s garnish
12. Basil Sprig garnish

Assembly

1. Form dough into 10 inch round
2. Spread GHO to cover round
3. Spread Mozzarella over GHO
4. Spread Sauce over Cheese
5. Place Ham slices
6. Place Kielbasa slices
7. Place Sausage crumbles
8. Place Pepper slices
9. Place Olive slices
10. Sprinkle Provolone over toppings

    Bake 12–15 minutes at 450 F until bread golden brown and cheese bubbling.
11. Garnish with Cherry Pepper/s
12. Garnish with Basil Sprig

Black Forest Ham - Prosciutto - Pesto Sauce - Asparagus - Mushroom

Toppings

1. Dough recipe of choice, 7 oz
2. Pesto Sauce, 2 oz
3. Fresh Mozzarella Cheese, 2½ oz
4. Goat Cheese, ½ oz
5. Black Forest Ham slices, 1½ oz
6. Prosciutto strips, 1 oz
7. Asparagus tips, 1½ oz
8. Sautéed Crimini Mushroom slices, 1 oz
9. Marinated Sun Dried Tomatoes julienne, 1 oz
10. Pitted Kalamata Olives, 9
11. Asiago Cheese, 1 oz
12. Basil Sprig garnish
13. Cherry Pepper/s garnish

Assembly

1. Form dough into 10 inch round
2. Spread Pesto to cover round
3. Spread Mozzarella over GHO
4. Fork Goat Cheese over Cheese
5. Place Ham strips
6. Place Prosciutto strips
7. Place Asparagus tips
8. Place Mushroom slices
9. Place Tomatoes julienne
10. Place Olives
11. Sprinkle Asiago over toppings

    Bake 12–15 minutes at 450 F until bread golden brown and cheese bubbling.

12. Garnish with Basil Sprig
13. Garnish with Cherry Pepper/s

Black Forest Ham & Grilled Chicken Sausage Omelette

Toppings

1. Dough recipe of choice, 7 oz
2. Garlic Herb Oil (GHO), 1 Tbsp
3. Fresh Mozzarella Cheese, 2 oz
4. Provolone Cheese, 1½ oz
5. Medium Eggs, 2
6. Black Forest Ham slices, 1½ oz
7. Grilled Chicken Sausage chunks, 1½ oz
8. Sautéed Button Mushroom slices, 1½ oz.
9. Red/Yellow Mini Pepper slices, ½ oz
10. Anaheim Chili slices, ½ oz
11. Parmigiano Reggiano Cheese, ½ oz
12. Basil sprig garnish
13. Cherry Pepper/s garnish

Assembly

1. Form dough into 10 inch round
2. Spread GHO to cover round
3. Spread Mozzarella over GHO
4. Spread Provolone over Mozzarella
5. Stir Eggs in bowl and pour over Cheese
6. Place Ham slices
7. Place Chicken chunks
8. Place Mushroom slices
9. Place Pepper strips
10. Place Chili slices
11. Sprinkle Parmigiano over toppings

    Bake 12–15 minutes at 450 F until bread golden brown and eggs set.

12. Garnish with Basil Sprig
13. Garnish with Cherry Pepper

Black Forest Ham - White, Green Asparagus - Artichoke Hearts

Toppings

1. Dough recipe of choice, 7 oz
2. Garlic Herb Oil (GHO), 1 Tbsp
3. Fresh Mozzarella Cheese, 3 oz
4. Tomato Sauce, 3 oz
5. Black Forest Ham slices, 2 oz
6. White/Green Asparagus tips, 1½ oz
7. Marinated Artichoke Heart wedges, 1½ oz
8. Pitted Kalamata Olives, 9
9. Provolone Cheese, 1 oz
10. Basil Sprig garnish
11. Cherry Pepper/s garnish

Assembly

1. Form dough into 10 inch round
2. Spread GHO to cover round
3. Spread Mozzarella over GHO
4. Spread Sauce over Cheese
5. Place Ham slices
6. Place Asparagus tips
7. Place Artichoke wedges
8. Place Olives
9. Sprinkle Provolone over toppings

   Bake 12–15 minutes at 450 F until bread golden brown and cheese bubbling.
10. Garnish with Basil Sprig
11. Garnish with Cherry Pepper/s

Chicken – Scalloped Potatoes au Gratin – Beans – Corn – Tomatoes

Toppings

1. Dough recipe of choice, 7 oz.
2. Garlic Herb Oil (GHO), 1 Tbsp
3. Fresh Mozzarella Cheese, 3 oz
4. Tomato Sauce, 3 oz
5. Scalloped Potatoes au Gratin slices, 2 oz
6. Grilled Chicken strips, 1½ oz
7. Black Beans/Corn mix, 1 oz
8. Baby Corn chunks, 8
9. Anaheim Chili slices, ½ oz
10. Grape Tomatoes, 9
11. Provolone Cheese, 1 oz
12. Cherry Pepper/s garnish
13. Pepperoncini garnish

Assembly

1. Form dough into 10 inch round
2. Spread GHO to cover round
3. Spread Mozzarella over GHO
4. Spread Sauce over Cheese
5. Place Potato slices
6. Place Chicken strips
7. Sprinkle B/Corn over toppings
8. Place Baby Corn chunks
9. Place Chili slices
10. Place Tomatoes
11. Sprinkle Provolone over toppings

    Bake 12–15 minutes at 450 F until bread golden brown and cheese bubbling.

12. Garnish with Cherry Pepper/s
13. Garnish with Pepperoncini

Chicken Breast - Sautéed Mushroom - Bell Pepper - Red Onion

Toppings

1. Dough recipe of choice, 7 oz
2. Garlic Herb Oil (GHO), 1 Tbsp
3. Smoked Mozzarella Cheese, 3 oz
4. Tomato Sauce, 3 oz
5. Grilled Chicken strips, 2 oz
6. Sautéed Button Mushroom slices, 1½ oz
7. Green/Red/Yellow Bell Pepper strips, 1½ oz
8. Red Onion slices, 1 oz
9. Provolone Cheese, 1 oz
10. Basil Sprig garnish

Assembly

1. Form dough into 10 inch round
2. Spread GHO to cover round
3. Spread Mozzarella over GHO
4. Spread Sauce over Cheese
5. Place Chicken strips
6. Place Mushroom slices
7. Place Pepper strips
8. Place Onion slices
9. Sprinkle Provolone over toppings

   Bake 12–15 minutes at 450 F until bread golden brown and cheese bubbling.

10. Garnish with Basil Sprig

Corn Beef – Country Dijon – Sauerkraut – Potato – Juniper Berries

Toppings

1. Rye Dough recipe, 7 oz.
2. Garlic Herb Oil (GHO), 1 Tbsp
3. Country Dijon Mustard, 2 oz
4. Mozzarella Cheese, 3 oz
5. Sautéed Potato slices, 2½ oz
6. Corn Beef shredded, 2½ oz
7. Sauerkraut with Juniper Berries, 2 oz
8. German/Swiss Cheese, 1 oz
9. Gherkin/s garnish

Assembly

1. Form dough into 10 inch round
2. Spread GHO to cover round
3. Spread Mustard over GHO
4. Spread Mozzarella over Mustard
5. Place Potato slices
6. Place Corn Beef
7. Spread Sauerkraut over toppings
8. Sprinkle Cheese over toppings

   Bake 12–15 minutes at 450 F until bread golden brown and cheese bubbling.

9. Garnish with Gherkin/s

Grilled Chicken - Hummus - Caramelized Onions - Mushrooms

Toppings

1. Dough recipe of choice, 7 oz
2. Garlic Herb Oil (GHO), 1 Tbsp
3. Hummus, 3 oz
4. Fresh Mozzarella Cheese, 3 oz
5. Grilled Chicken strips, 2 oz
6. Sautéed Crimini Mushrooms slices, 1½ oz
7. Caramelized Onions, 1 oz
8. Red/Yellow Mini Pepper slices, ½ oz
9. Anaheim Chili slices, ½ oz
10. Roasted Garlic cloves, ½ oz
11. Provolone Cheese, 1 oz
12. Cherry Pepper/s garnish
13. Pepperoncini

Assembly

1. Form dough into 10 inch round
2. Spread GHO to lightly cover round
3. Spread Hummus over dough
4. Spread Mozzarella over GHO
5. Place Chicken strips
6. Place Mushroom slices
7. Place Caramelized Onions
8. Place Pepper slices
9. Place Chili slices
10. Garlic cloves
11. Sprinkle Provolone over toppings

    Bake 12–15 minutes at 450 F until bread golden brown and cheese bubbling.

12. Garnish with Cherry Pepper/s
13. Garnish with Pepperoncini

Grilled Chicken Sausage - Artichoke Hearts - Pepper - Olive

Toppings

1. Dough recipe of choice, 7 oz
2. Garlic Herb Oil (GHO), 1 Tbsp
3. Mozzarella Cheese, 3 oz
4. Tomato Sauce, 3 oz
5. Grilled Chicken Sausage chunks, 2½ oz
6. Marinated Artichoke Heart wedges, 1½ oz
7. Red Mini Pepper slices, 1 oz
8. Black Olive slices, 1 oz
9. Provolone Cheese, 1 oz
10. Basil Sprig garnish
11. Cherry Pepper/s garnish

Assembly

1. Form dough into 10 inch round
2. Spread GHO to cover round
3. Spread Mozzarella over GHO
4. Spread Sauce over Cheese
5. Place Chicken chunks
6. Place Artichoke wedges
7. Place Pepper slices
8. Place Olive slices
9. Sprinkle Provolone over toppings

   Bake 12–15 minutes at 450 F until bread golden brown and cheese bubbling.

10. Garnish with Basil sprig
11. Garnish with Cherry Pepper/s

Grilled Chicken - Sautéed Mushroom - Broccoli - Pepper - Olive

Toppings

1. Dough recipe of choice, 7 oz
2. Garlic Herb Oil (GHO), 1 Tbsp
3. Fresh Mozzarella Cheese, 3 oz
4. Tomato Sauce, 3 oz
5. Grilled Chicken strips, 2 oz
6. Sautéed Button Mushroom slices, 1½ oz
7. Broccoli florets, 1½ oz
8. Red/Yellow Mini Pepper slices, ½ oz
9. Black Olive slices, ½ oz
10. Provolone Cheese, 1 oz
11. Cherry Pepper/s garnish

Assembly

1. Form dough into 10 inch round
2. Spread GHO to lightly cover round
3. Spread Mozzarella over Sauce
4. Spread Sauce over dough
5. Place Chicken strips
6. Place Mushroom slices
7. Place Broccoli florets
8. Place Pepper slices
9. Place Olive slices
10. Sprinkle Provolone over toppings

    Bake 12–15 minutes at 450 F until bread golden brown and cheese bubbling.

11. Garnish with Cherry Pepper/s

Kielbasa - Bacon - Corn - Black Beans - Mini Pepper

Toppings

1. Dough recipe of choice, 7 oz.
2. Garlic Herb Oil (GHO), 1 Tbsp
3. Mozzarella Cheese, 2½ oz
4. Tomato Sauce, 3 oz
5. Grilled Kielbasa slices, 2½ oz
6. Cooked Bacon strips, 1 oz
7. Anaheim Chili slices, ½ oz
8. Red/Yellow Mini Pepper slices, ½ oz
9. Red Onion slices, ½ oz
10. Corn/Black Bean mix, 1 oz
11. Smoked Gouda, 1 oz
12. Pecorino Romano Cheese, ½ oz
13. Cherry Pepper/s garnish

Assembly

1. Form dough into 10 inch round
2. Spread GHO to cover round
3. Spread Mozzarella over GHO
4. Spread Sauce over Cheese
5. Place Kielbasa slices
6. Place Bacon strips
7. Place Chili strips
8. Place Pepper slices
9. Place Onion slices
10. Sprinkle Corn/Bean mix over toppings
11. Sprinkle Gouda over toppings
12. Sprinkle Pecorino over toppings

    Bake 12–15 minutes at 450 F until bread golden brown and cheese bubbling.
13. Garnish with Cherry Pepper/s

Meatballs - Bacon - Tomatoes - Pepper - Anaheim Chili - Onion

Toppings

1. Dough recipe of choice, 7 oz.
2. Garlic Herb Oil (GHO), 1 Tbsp
3. Mozzarella Cheese, 3 oz
4. Tomato Sauce, 3 oz
5. Meatball quarters, 2 oz
6. Cooked Bacon strips, 1 oz
7. Grape Tomatoes, 9
8. Yellow Mini Pepper slices, ½ oz
9. Anaheim chilies, ½ oz
10. Red Onion slices, ½ oz
11. Provolone Cheese, 1 oz
12. Basil Sprig garnish
13. Pepperoncini garnish

Assembly

1. Form dough into 10 inch round
2. Spread GHO to cover round
3. Spread Mozzarella over GHO
4. Spread Sauce over Cheese
5. Place Meatball quarters
6. Place Bacon strips
7. Place Tomatoes
8. Place Pepper slices
9. Place Chili slices
10. Place Onion slices
11. Spread Provolone over toppings
    Bake 12–15 minutes at 450 F until bread golden brown and cheese bubbling.
12. Garnish with Basil Sprig
13. Garnish with Pepperoncini

Meatball - Mushroom - Tomatoes - Anaheim Chili - Mini Peppers

Toppings

1. Dough recipe of choice, 7 oz.
2. Garlic Herb Oil (GHO), 1 Tbsp
3. Fresh Mozzarella Cheese, 2½ oz
4. Tomato Sauce, 3 oz
5. Meatball quarters, 2 oz
6. Roma Tomato slices, 6
7. Sautéed Button Mushroom slices, 1 oz
8. Yellow/Orange Mini Pepper slices, ½ oz
9. Anaheim Chili slices, ½ oz
10. Provolone Cheese, 1 oz
11. Parmesan Cheese, ½ oz
12. Basil Sprig garnish
13. Cherry Pepper/s garnish

Assembly

1. Form dough into 10 inch round
2. Spread GHO to cover round
3. Spread Mozzarella over GHO
4. Spread Sauce over Cheese
5. Place Meatball quarters
6. Place Tomato slices
7. Place Mushroom slices
8. Place Pepper slices
9. Place Chili slices
10. Sprinkle Provolone over toppings
11. Sprinkle Parmesan Cheese over toppings

    Bake 12–15 minutes at 450 F until bread golden brown and cheese bubbling.

12. Garnish with Basil Sprig
13. Garnish with Cherry Pepper/s

Meatball - Tomato Sauce - Corn - Black Beans - Pepper

Toppings

1. Dough recipe of choice, 7 oz.
2. Garlic Herb Oil (GHO), 1 Tbsp
3. Mozzarella Cheese, 2½ oz
4. Tomato Sauce, 3 oz
5. Meatball quarters, 2½ oz
6. Cooked Bacon strips, 1 oz
7. Anaheim Chili slices, ½ oz
8. Red/Yellow Mini Pepper slices, ½ oz
9. Corn/Black Bean mix, 1½ oz
10. Provolone Cheese, 1 oz
11. Pecorino Romano Cheese, ½ oz
12. Cherry Pepper/s garnish

Assembly

1. Form dough into 10 inch round
2. Spread GHO to cover round
3. Spread Mozzarella over GHO
4. Spread Sauce over Cheese
5. Place Meatball quarters
6. Place Bacon strips
7. Place Chili slices
8. Place Pepper slices
9. Sprinkle Corn/Bean mix over toppings
10. Sprinkle Provolone over toppings
11. Sprinkle Pecorino over toppings

    Bake 12–15 minutes at 450 F until bread golden brown and cheese bubbling.

12. Garnish with Cherry Pepper/s

Omelette - Broccoli - Spinach - Mushrooms - Tomatoes - Peppers

Toppings

1. Dough recipe of choice, 7 oz
2. Garlic Herb Oil (GHO), 1 Tbsp
3. Fresh Mozzarella Cheese, 3 ½ oz
4. Medium Eggs, 2
5. Sautéed Spinach, 1½ oz
6. Broccoli florets, 1½ oz
7. Sautéed Button Mushroom slices, 1½ oz
8. Grape Tomatoes, 9
9. Yellow Mini Pepper slices, 1 oz
10. Parmigiano Reggiano Cheese, ½ oz
11. Cherry Pepper/s garnish
12. Basil Sprig garnish

Assembly

1. Form dough into 10 inch round
2. Spread GHO to cover round
3. Spread Mozzarella over GHO
4. Stir Eggs in bowl and pour over Cheese
5. Spread Spinach over toppings
6. Place Broccoli florets
7. Place Mushroom slices
8. Place Tomatoes
9. Place Pepper slices
10. Sprinkle Parmigiano over toppings

    Bake 12–15 minutes at 450 F until bread golden brown and eggs set.

11. Garnish with Cherry Pepper/s
12. Garnish with Basil Sprig

Omelette - Sausage - Onion - Mini Pepper - Anaheim Chili

Toppings

1. Dough recipe of choice, 7 oz
2. Garlic Herb Oil (GHO), 1 Tbsp
3. Fresh Mozzarella Cheese, 3½ oz
4. Medium eggs, 2
5. Sausage crumbles, 2½ oz
6. Grilled Onion slices, 1 oz
7. Red/Yellow Mini Pepper slices, ½ oz
8. Anaheim chili slices, ½ oz
9. Parmesan Cheese, ½ oz
10. Cherry Pepper/s garnish
11. Pepperoncini garnish

Assembly

1. Form dough into 10 inch round
2. Spread GHO to cover round
3. Spread Mozzarella over GHO
4. Stir Eggs in bowl and pour over Cheese
5. Place Sausage crumbles
6. Place Onion slices
7. Place Pepper slices
8. Place Chili slices
9. Sprinkle Parmesan over toppings

    Bake 12–15 minutes at 450 F until bread golden brown and eggs set.

10. Garnish with Cherry Pepper/s
11. Garnish with Pepperoncini

Sausage - Tomatoes - Japanese Eggplant - Mini Peppers - Chili

Toppings

1. Dough recipe of choice, 7 oz
2. Garlic Herb Oil (GHO), 1 Tbsp
3. Fresh Mozzarella Cheese, 3 oz
4. Tomato Sauce, 3 oz
5. Grilled Japanese Eggplant slices, 1½ oz
6. Italian Sausage crumbles, 2 oz
7. Yellow Mini Pepper slices, ½ oz
8. Anaheim Chili slices, ½ oz
9. Grape Tomatoes, 9
10. Provolone Cheese, 1 oz
11. Basil Sprig garnish

Assembly

1. Form dough into 10 inch round
2. Spread GHO to cover round
3. Spread Mozzarella over GHO
4. Spread Sauce over Cheese
5. Place Eggplant slices
6. Place Sausage crumbles
7. Place Pepper slices
8. Place Chili slices
9. Place Tomatoes
10. Sprinkle Provolone over toppings

    Bake 12–15 minutes at 450 F until bread golden brown and cheese bubbling.

11. Garnish with Basil Sprig

Sausage - Tomato Sauce - Bell Pepper - Onion - Chili - Pepperoncini

Toppings

1. Dough recipe of choice, 7 oz
2. Garlic Herb Oil (GHO), 1 Tbsp
3. Mozzarella Cheese, 2½ oz
4. Tomato Sauce, 3 oz
5. Grilled link Sausage strips sliced in half lengthwise, 2½ oz
6. Red/Yellow Bell Pepper strips, 1 oz
7. Anaheim Chili strips, 1 oz
8. Grilled Onion slices, 1 oz
9. Pepperoncini strips, ½ oz
10. Provolone Cheese, 1 oz
11. Pecorino Romano, ½ oz
12. Cherry Pepper/s garnish

Assembly

1. Form dough into 10 inch round
2. Spread GHO to cover round
3. Spread Mozzarella over GHO
4. Spread Sauce over Cheese
5. Place Sausage strips
6. Place Pepper strips
7. Place Chili strips
8. Place Onion slices
9. Place Pepperoncini strips
10. Sprinkle Provolone over toppings
11. Sprinkle Pecorino over toppings

    Bake 12–15 minutes at 450 F until bread golden brown and cheese bubbling.

12. Garnish with Cherry Pepper/s

Sausage - White Sauce - Sautéed Mushroom - Mini Pepper

Toppings

1. Dough recipe of choice, 7 oz
2. Garlic Herb Oil (GHO), 1 Tbsp
3. White Sauce, 4 oz (see recipe)
4. Sausage crumbles, 2½ oz
5. Sautéed Button Mushroom slices, 1½ oz
6. Grilled Red/Yellow Mini Pepper strips, 1½ oz
7. Grilled Onion strips, 1 oz
8. Pecorino Romano, ½ oz

Assembly

1. Form dough into 10 inch round
2. Spread GHO to cover round
3. Mix Sauce, Sausage crumbles,
4. Place Mushroom slices, Pepper strips and Onion strips in bowl, empty and spread over dough round.
5. Sprinkle Pecorino over toppings

   Bake 12–15 minutes at 450 F until bread golden brown and cheese bubbling

Scalloped Potatoes au Gratin – Mushroom – Spinach – Grilled Pepper

Toppings

1. Dough recipe of choice, 7 oz
2. Garlic Herb Oil (GHO), 1 Tbsp
3. Fresh Mozzarella Cheese, 2½ oz
4. Sautéed Spinach, 1½ oz
5. Scalloped Potatoes au Gratin, 2½ oz
6. Grilled Red/Orange Bell Pepper strips, 1½ oz
7. Sautéed Button Mushroom slices, 1 oz
8. Provolone Cheese, 1 oz
9. Pecorino Romano Cheese, ½ oz
10. Cherry Pepper/s garnish

Assembly

1. Form dough into 10 inch round
2. Spread GHO to cover round
3. Spread Mozzarella over GHO
4. Spread Spinach over toppings
5. Place Potato slices
6. Place Pepper strips
7. Place Mushroom slices
8. Sprinkle Cheese over toppings
9. Sprinkle Pecorino over toppings

   Bake 12–15 minutes at 450 F until bread golden brown and cheese bubbling.

10. Garnish with Cherry Pepper/s

Scalloped Potatoes au Gratin Omellete

Toppings

1. Dough recipe of choice, 7 oz.
2. Garlic Herb Oil (GHO), 1 Tbsp
3. Fresh Mozzarella Cheese, 3½ oz
4. Medium eggs stirred together, 2
5. Scalloped Potatoes au Gratin, 2½ oz
6. Sausage crumbles, 1½ oz
7. Bacon strips, ½ oz
8. Caramelized Onions, 1 oz
9. Grape Tomatoes, 9
10. Red/Yellow Mini Pepper slices, ½ oz
11. Pecorino Romano, ½ oz
12. Cherry Pepper/s garnish

Assembly

1. Form dough into 10 inch round
2. Spread GHO to cover round
3. Spread Mozzarella over GHO
4. Pour Eggs over toppings
5. Place Potato slices
6. Place Sausage crumbles
7. Place Bacon strips
8. Spread Onions
9. Place Tomatoes
10. Place Pepper slices
11. Sprinkle Pecorino over toppings

    Bake 12–15 minutes at 450 F until bread golden brown and eggs set.
12. Garnish with Cherry Pepper/s

Shrimp & Chicken Pizza Salad - Lettuce - Tomato - Avocado

Toppings

1. Dough recipe of choice, 7 oz
2. Garlic Herb Oil (GHO), 1 Tbsp
3. Fresh Mozzarella Cheese, 3 oz
4. Tomato Sauce, 3 oz
5. Shrimp (31/40 ct. per lb.) butterflied and brushed with GHO & Lemon Juice, 6
6. Grilled Chicken strips, 1½ oz
7. Blue Cheese crumbles, 1 oz
8. Romaine Lettuce to taste
9. Roma Tomato thin slices, 7
10. Grape Tomatoes, 6
11. Black Olive slices, 1 oz
12. Avocado slices, 6

Assembly

1. Form dough into 10 inch round
2. Spread GHO to cover round
3. Spread Mozzarella over GHO
4. Spread Sauce over Cheese
5. Place Shrimp
6. Place Chicken strips
7. Place Blue Cheese crumbles

   Bake 12–15 minutes at 450 F until bread golden brown and cheese bubbling.

8. Place in bowl Lettuce, Tomato slices, Tomatoes and Olive slices. Toss in lightly applied Vinaigrette and empty over toppings.
9. Place Avocado slices. Serve immediately.

Steak - Tomatoes - Sautéed Mushrooms - Bell Pepper - Onion

Toppings

1. Dough recipe of choice, 7 oz
2. Garlic Herb Oil (GHO), 1 Tbsp
3. Mozzarella Cheese, 3 oz
4. Tomato Sauce, 3 oz
5. Seared Steak strips, 2 oz
6. Sautéed Crimini Mushroom slices, 1 oz
7. Grilled Onion slices, 1 oz
8. Grape Tomatoes, 9
9. Anaheim Chili slices, ½ oz
10. Red/Yellow Mini Pepper slices, ½ oz
11. Provolone Cheese, 1 oz
12. Pepperoncini garnish
13. Cherry Pepper/s garnish

Assembly

1. Form dough into 10 inch round
2. Spread GHO to cover round
3. Spread Mozzarella over GHO
4. Spread Sauce over Cheese
5. Place Steak strips
6. Place Mushroom slices
7. Place Onion slices
8. Place Tomatoes
9. Place Chili slices
10. Place Pepper slices
11. Sprinkle Provolone over toppings

    Bake 12–15 minutes at 450 F until bread golden brown and cheese bubbling.

12. Garnish with Pepperoncini
13. Garnish with Cherry Pepper/s

Eggplant Parmigiana - Bell Pepper - Tomato - Kalamata Olives

Toppings

1. Dough recipe of choice, 7 oz
2. Garlic Herb Oil (GHO), 1 Tbsp
3. Fresh Mozzarella Cheese, 2 ½ oz.
4. Goat Cheese, ½ oz
5. Tomato Sauce, 3 oz
6. Eggplant Parmigiana wedges, 2 oz
7. Grilled Yellow Bell Pepper strips, 1½ oz
8. Marinated Sun Dried Tomatoes julienne, 1 oz
9. Pitted Kalamata Olives, 9
10. Provolone Cheese, ½ oz
11. Parmesan Cheese, ½ oz
12. Basil Sprig garnish
13. Cherry Pepper/s garnish

Assembly

1. Form dough into 10 inch round
2. Spread GHO to cover round
3. Spread Mozzarella over GHO
4. Fork Goat Cheese over Mozzarella
5. Spread Sauce over Cheese
6. Place Eggplant wedges
7. Place Pepper strips
8. Place Tomatoes julienne
9. Place Olives
10. Sprinkle Provolone over toppings
11. Sprinkle Parmesan over toppings

    Bake 12–15 minutes at 450 F until bread golden brown and cheese bubbling.

12. Garnish with Basil
13. Garnish with Pepper/s

Ham – Eggplant Parmigiana – Artichoke Hearts – Grilled Pepper

Toppings

1. Dough recipe of choice, 7 oz
2. Garlic Herb Oil (GHO), 1 Tbsp
3. Fresh Mozzarella Cheese, 2½ oz.
4. Tomato Sauce, 3 oz
5. Black Forest Ham strips, 1½ oz
6. Eggplant Parmigiana slices, 1½ oz
7. Grilled Mini Pepper strips, 1 oz
8. Marinated Artichoke Heart wedges, 1 oz
9. Pitted Kalamata Olives, 9
10. Provolone Cheese, 1 oz
11. Parmesan Cheese, ½ oz
12. Cherry Pepper/s garnish
13. Pepperoncini garnish

Assembly

1. Form dough into 10 inch round
2. Spread GHO to cover round
3. Spread Mozzarella over GHO
4. Spread Sauce over Cheese
5. Place Ham strips
6. Place Eggplant slices
7. Place Pepper strips
8. Place Artichoke wedges
9. Place Olives
10. Sprinkle Provolone over toppings
11. Sprinkle Parmesan over toppings

   Bake 12–15 minutes at 450 F until bread golden brown and cheese bubbling.

12. Garnish with Cherry Pepper/s
13. Garnish with Pepperoncini

Meatball - Polenta - Baby Corn - Mini Pepper - Chili

Toppings

1. Dough recipe of choice, 7 oz.
2. Garlic Herb Oil (GHO), 1 Tbsp
3. Fresh Mozzarella Cheese 3 oz
4. Tomato Sauce, 3 oz
5. Meatball quarters, 2 oz
6. Grilled Red Onion slices, 1 oz
7. Grilled Polenta strips, 1 oz
8. Baby Corn chunks, 1 oz
9. Red/Yellow Mini Pepper slices, ½ oz
10. Anaheim Chili slices, ½ oz
11. Provolone Cheese, 1 oz
12. Basil Sprig garnish
13. Cherry Pepper/s garnish

Assembly

1. Form dough into 10 inch round
2. Spread GHO to cover round
3. Spread Mozzarella over GHO
4. Spread Sauce over Cheese
5. Place Meatball quarters
6. Sprinkle Onion over toppings
7. Place Polenta strips
8. Place Corn chunks
9. Place Pepper slices
10. Place Chili slices
11. Sprinkle Provolone over toppings

    Bake 12–15 minutes at 450 F until bread golden brown and cheese bubbling.

12. Garnish with Basil Sprig
13. Garnish with Cherry Pepper/s

Pepperoni - Sausage - Tomatoes - Pepper - Chili - Onion - Olive

Toppings

1. Dough recipe of choice, 7 oz
2. Garlic Herb Oil (GHO), 1 Tbsp
3. Mozzarella Cheese, 2½ oz
4. Tomato Sauce, 3 oz
5. Pepperoni slices, 1 oz
6. Cooked Hot Italian Sausage crumbles, 1½ oz
7. Yellow Mini Pepper slices, ½ oz
8. Anaheim Chili slices, ½ oz
9. Grape Tomatoes, 9
10. Red onion slices, ½ oz.
11. Black Olive slices, ½ oz
12. Provolone Cheese, 1 oz
13. Basil Sprig garnish
14. Pepperoncini garnish

Assembly

1. Form dough into 10 inch round
2. Spread GHO to cover round
3. Spread Mozzarella over GHO
4. Spread Sauce over Cheese
5. Place Pepperoni slices
6. Place Sausage crumbles
7. Place Pepper slices
8. Place Chili slices
9. Place Tomatoes
10. Place Onion slices
11. Place Olive slices
12. Sprinkle Provo over toppings
    Bake 12–15 minutes at 450 F until bread golden brown and cheese bubbling.
13. Garnish with Basil Sprig
14. Garnish with Pepperoncini

Pizza Margherita

Toppings

1. Dough recipe of choice, 7 oz
2. Garlic Herb Oil (GHO), 1 Tbsp
3. Fresh Basil leaves
4. Fresh Mozzarella Cheese, 4 oz
5. Tomato Sauce, 3 oz
6. Grape Tomatoes, 10
7. Basil Sprig/s garnish

Assembly

1. Form dough into 10 inch round
2. Spread GHO to cover round
3. Spread Basil leaves over GHO
4. Spread Mozzarella over Basil leaves
5. Spread Sauce over Cheese
6. Place Tomatoes

   Bake 12–15 minutes at 450 F until bread golden brown and cheese bubbling.

7. Garnish with Basil sprig/s

Pizza Ham, Egg, Tomato & Avocado Salad

Toppings

1. Dough recipe of choice, 7 oz
2. Garlic Herb Oil (GHO), 1 Tbsp
3. Fresh Mozzarella Cheese, 3 oz
4. Gorgonzola Cheese, 1 oz
5. Ham slices, 2 oz
6. Boiled Egg (2) slices & crumbles
7. Romaine Lettuce to taste
8. Roma Tomato thin slices, 7
9. Grape Tomatoes, 6
10. Black Olive slices, 1 oz
11. Avocado slices, 6

Assembly

1. Form dough into 10 inch round
2. Spread GHO to cover round
3. Spread Mozzarella over GHO
4. Spread Gorgonzola over Mozzarella
5. Place Ham slices
6. Place Egg slices

   Bake 12–15 minutes at 450 F until bread golden brown and cheese bubbling.

7. Place in bowl Lettuce, Tomato slices, Grape Tomatoes and Olive slices. Toss in lightly applied Vinaigrette and empty over toppings.
8. Place Avocado slices. Serve immediately.

Prosciutto - Pesto Sauce - Asparagus - Walnuts - Goat Cheese

Toppings

1. Dough recipe of choice, 7 oz.
2. Pesto Sauce, 2 oz
3. Fresh Mozzarella Cheese, 2½ oz
4. Goat Cheese, ½ oz
5. Prosciutto strips, 1½ oz
6. Asparagus tips, 2 oz
7. Grilled Yellow Bell Pepper strips, 1 oz
8. Walnut quarters, 1oz
9. Fontina Cheese, 1 oz.
10. Basil Sprig garnish
11. Cherry Pepper/s garnish

Assembly

1. Form dough into 10 inch round
2. Spread Sauce over round
3. Spread Mozzarella over Sauce
4. Fork Goat Cheese over Mozzarella
5. Place Prosciutto strips
6. Place Asparagus tips
7. Place Pepper strips
8. Sprinkle Walnut quarters over toppings
9. Sprinkle Fontina over toppings

   Bake 12–15 minutes at 450 F until bread golden brown and cheese bubbling.

10. Place Basil Sprig
11. Garnish with Cherry Pepper/s

Salami - Eggplant Parmigiana - Bell Pepper - Tomato - Olive

Toppings

1. Dough recipe of choice, 7 oz
2. Garlic Herb Oil (GHO), 1 Tbsp
3. Mozzarella Cheese, 2½ oz
4. Tomato Sauce, 3 oz
5. Salami slices, 1½ oz
6. Green Bell Pepper slices, 6
7. Roma Tomato thin slices, 6
8. Eggplant Parmigina quarters, 1½ oz
9. Black Olive slices, 1 oz
10. Provolone Cheese, 1 oz
11. Parmesan Cheese, ½ oz
12. Cherry Pepper/s garnish
13. Pepperoncini

Assembly

1. Form dough into 10 inch round
2. Spread GHO to cover round
3. Spread Mozzarella over GHO
4. Spread Sauce over Cheese
5. Place Salami slices
6. Place Pepper slices
7. Place Tomato slices
8. Place Eggplant quarters
9. Place Olive slices
10. Sprinkle Provolone over toppings
11. Sprinkle Parmesan over toppings

   Bake 12–15 minutes at 450 F until bread golden brown and cheese bubbling.

12. Garnish with Cherry Pepper/s
13. Garnish with Pepperoncini

Salami - Grilled Zucchini - Grilled Mini Pepper - Kalamata Olives

Toppings

1. Dough recipe of choice, 7 oz
2. Garlic Herb Oil (GHO), 1 Tbsp
3. Mozzarella Cheese, 2½ oz
4. Goat Cheese, ½ oz
5. Tomato Sauce, 3 oz
6. Salami slices, 1½ oz
7. Grilled Zucchini strips, 1½ oz
8. Grilled Red/Yellow Mini Pepper strips, 1½ oz
9. Pitted Kalamata Olives, 9
10. Provolone Cheese, 1 oz
11. Cherry Pepper/s garnish
12. Basil sprig garnish
13. Pepperoncini garnish

Assembly

1. Form dough into 10 inch round
2. Spread GHO to lightly cover round
3. Spread Mozzarella over GHO
4. Fork Goat over Mozzarella
5. Spread Sauce over Cheese
6. Place Salami slices
7. Place Zucchini strips
8. Place Pepper strips
9. Place Olives
10. Sprinkle Provolone over toppings

    Bake 12–15 minutes at 450 F until bread golden brown and cheese bubbling.
11. Garnish with Cherry Pepper/s
12. Garnish with Basil Sprig
13. Garnish with Pepperoncini

Spinach - Ham - Mushrooms - Tomatoes - Olives

Toppings

1. Rye dough recipe, 7 oz
2. Garlic Herb Oil (GHO), 1 Tbsp
3. Fresh Mozzarella Cheese, 2½ oz
4. Tomato Sauce, 3 oz
5. Sautéed Spinach, 1½ oz
6. Ham slices, 2 oz
7. Roma Tomato thin slices, 7
8. Sautéed Mushroom slices, 1 oz
9. Black Olive slices, ½ oz
10. Provolone Cheese, 1 oz
11. Pecorino Romano Cheese, ½ oz
12. Cherry Pepper/s garnish
13. Pepperocini garnish

Assembly

1. Form dough into 10 inch round
2. Spread GHO to cover round
3. Spread Mozzarella over GHO
4. Spread Sauce over Cheese
5. Spread Spinach over toppings
6. Place Ham slices
7. Place Tomato slices
8. Place Mushroom slices
9. Place Olive slices
10. Sprinkle Provolone over toppings
11. Sprinkle Pecorino over toppings

    Bake 12–15 minutes at 450 F until bread golden brown and cheese bubbling.

12. Garnish with Cherry Pepper/s
13. Garnish with Pepperoncini

Tomato - Pesto Sauce - Asparagus - Yellow Squash - Cauliflower

Toppings

1. Dough recipe of choice, 7 oz
2. Pesto Sauce, 2 oz
3. Mozzarella Cheese, 2 oz
4. Goat Cheese, ½ oz
5. Asparagus tips, 1½ oz
6. Roma Tomato thin slices, 7
7. Grilled Yellow Squash slices, 1½ oz
8. Cauliflower florets, 1½ oz
9. Olive slices, ½ oz
10. Pine Nuts, ½ oz
11. Provolone Cheese, 1 oz
12. Parmesan, ½ oz
13. Basil Sprig garnish

Assembly

1. Form dough into 10 inch round
2. Spread Pesto Sauce over round
3. Spread Mozzarella over GHO
4. Fork Goat Cheese over Cheese
5. Place Asparagus tips
6. Place Tomato slices
7. Place Squash slices
8. Place Cauliflower florets
9. Place Olive slices
10. Sprinkle Nuts over toppings
11. Sprinkle Provolone over toppings
12. Sprinkle Parmesan over toppings

   Bake 12–15 minutes at 450 F until bread golden brown and cheese bubbling.

13. Garnish with Basil Sprig

Carnitas Santa Fe

Toppings

1. Dough recipe of choice, 7 oz
2. Garlic Herb Oil (GHO), 1 Tbsp
3. Cilantro to taste
4. Smoked Mozzarella, 2 oz Cheddar Cheese, 1 oz
5. Medium Chunky Salsa, 4 oz
6. Roasted Pork shredded, 2 oz
7. Anaheim Chile slices, ½ oz
8. Red/Yellow Mini Pepper slices, ½ oz
9. Red Onion slices, 1 oz
10. Black Olive slices, 1 oz
11. Monterey Jack, 1 oz
12. Avocado slice/s garnish
13. Cherry Pepper/s garnish

Assembly

1. Form dough into 10 inch round
2. Spread GHO to cover round
3. Sprinkle Cilantro over GHO
4. Spread Mozzarella/Cheddar over GHO
5. Spread Salsa over Cheese
6. Place shredded Pork
7. Place Chili slices
8. Place Pepper slices
9. Place Onion slices
10. Place Olive slices
11. Sprinkle Jack over toppings

    Bake 12–15 minutes at 450 F until bread golden brown and cheese bubbling.

12. Garnish with Avocado slice/s
13. Garnish with Cherry Pepper/s

Chicken - Salsa - Chorizo - Red Corn - Tomato - Jalapeno

Toppings

1. Masa Harina dough recipe, 7 oz
2. Garlic Herb Oil (GHO), 1 Tbsp
3. Smoked Mozzarella Cheese, 2 oz
   Cheddar, 1 oz
4. Salsa, 4 oz
5. Grilled Chicken Breast strips, 1 oz
6. Cooked Chorizo crumbles, 1 oz
7. Red/Yellow Tomato slices, 1½ oz
8. Fresh Red Corn kernels, 1 oz
9. Jalapeno slices, ½ oz
10. Monterey Jack Cheese, 1 oz
11. Avocado half garnish
12. Cherry Pepper garnish

Assembly

1. Form dough into 10 inch round
2. Spread GHO to cover round
3. Spread Mozzarella/Cheddar over GHO
4. Spread Salsa over Cheese
5. Place Chicken strips
6. Place Chorizo crumbles
7. Place Tomato slices
8. Sprinkle Corn kernels over toppings
9. Place Jalapeno slices
10. Sprinkle Monterey Jack over toppings

    Bake 12–15 minutes at 450 F until
    bread golden brown and cheese
    bubbling.

11. Garnish with Avocado half
12. Garnish with Cherry Pepper

Chicken Fajitas

Toppings

1. Dough recipe of choice, 7 oz
2. Garlic Herb Oil (GHO), 1 Tbsp
3. Cilantro to taste
4. Mozzarella, 2 oz/Cheddar Cheese, 1 oz
5. Medium Chunky Salsa, 4 oz
6. Grilled Chicken Breast strips, 2 oz
7. Anaheim Chile slices, ½ oz
8. Red/Yellow Mini Pepper slices, ½ oz
9. Red Onion slices, 1 oz
10. Black Olive slices, 1 oz
11. Monterey Jack Cheese, 1 oz
12. Avocado slice/s garnish
13. Cherry Pepper/s garnish

Assembly

1. Form dough into 10 inch round
2. Spread GHO to cover round
3. Sprinkle Cilantro over GHO
4. Spread Mozzarella/Cheddar over GHO
5. Spread Salsa over Cheese
6. Place Chicken strips
7. Place Chili slices
8. Place Pepper slices
9. Place Onion slices
10. Place Olive slices
11. Sprinkle Monterey Jack over toppings

    Bake 12–15 minutes at 450 F until bread golden brown and cheese bubbling.

12. Garnish with Avocado slice/s
13. Garnish with Cherry Pepper/s

Pork ~ Salsa ~ Black Beans ~ Anaheim Chilies ~ Grape Tomatoes

Toppings

1. Dough recipe of choice, 7 oz.
2. Garlic Herb Oil (GHO), 1 Tbsp
3. Fresh Cilantro to taste
4. Smoked Mozzarella Cheese, 3 oz
5. Medium Chunky Salsa, 4 oz
6. Roasted Pork shredded, 2 oz
7. Black Beans, 1½ oz
8. Anaheim Chile slices, ½ oz
9. Cherry Tomatoes halves, 12
10. Monterey Jack Cheese, 1 oz
11. Avocado slice/s garnish

Assembly

1. Form dough into 10 inch round
2. Spread GHO to cover round
3. Sprinkle Cilantro over GHO
4. Spread Mozzarella over GHO
5. Spread Salsa over Cheese
6. Place shredded Pork
7. Sprinkle Beans over toppings
8. Place Chili slices
9. Place Tomato halves
10. Sprinkle Jack over toppings

    Bake 12–15 minutes at 450 F until bread golden brown and cheese bubbling.

11. Garnish with Avocado slice/s

Pizza Mexicana

Toppings

1. Dough recipe of choice, 7 oz
2. Garlic Herb Oil (GHO), 1 Tbsp
3. Refried Beans, 2 oz
4. Smoked Mozzarella Cheese, 2 oz
5. Roasted Pork shredded, 1 ½ oz
6. Enchilada Sauce, 2 oz
7. Baby Corn Chunks, 1 oz
8. Anaheim Chile slices, ½ oz
9. Orange Mini Pepper slices, ½ oz
10. Grape Tomatoes, 9
11. Black Olive slices, ½ oz
12. Cheddar, 1 oz/Monterey Jack Cheese 1 oz
13. Tortilla chips/Guacamole garnish
14. Cherry Pepper/s garnish

Assembly

1. Form dough into 10 inch round
2. Spread GHO to cover round
3. Spread Beans over GHO
4. Spread Mozzarella over Beans
5. Place shredded Pork
6. Spread Enchilada Sauce over toppings
7. Place Corn chunks
8. Place Chili slices
9. Place Pepper slices
10. Place Tomatoes
11. Sprinkle Olive slices over toppings
12. Spread Cheddar/Jack over toppings

    Bake 12–15 minutes at 450 F until bread golden brown and cheese bubbling.
13. Garnish with Chips/Guacamole
14. Garnish with Cherry Pepper

Thin Crust Pizza—Rancho Grande **153**

Shrimp Santa Fe

Toppings

1. Dough recipe of choice, 7 oz
2. Garlic Herb Oil (GHO), 1 Tbsp
3. Cilantro to taste
4. Mozzarella Cheese, 2 oz Cheddar, 1 oz
5. Medium Chunky Salsa, 4 oz
6. Shrimp (31/40 ct. per lb) butterflied and brushed with GHO & Lemon Juice, 8
7. Corn/Black Bean/Red Onion mix, 1½ oz
8. Red Mini Pepper slices, ½ oz
9. Anaheim Chili slices, ½ oz
10. Black Olive slices, ½ oz
11. Monterey Jack Cheese, 1 oz
12. Avocado slice/s garnish
13. Cherry Pepper/s garnish

Assembly

1. Form dough into 10 inch round
2. Spread GHO to cover round
3. Sprinkle Cilantro over GHO
4. Spread Cheese over round
5. Spread Salsa over Cheese
6. Place Shrimp
7. Sprinkle C/BB/RO mix over top
8. Place Pepper slices
9. Place Chili slices
10. Sprinkle Olive slices over top
11. Sprinkle Jack over toppings

    Bake 12–15 minutes at 450 F until bread golden brown and cheese bubbling.

12. Garnish with Avocado slice/s
13. Garnish with Cherry Pepper/s

Surf & Turf Veracruz

Toppings

1. Dough recipe of choice, 7 oz.
2. Garlic Herb Oil (GHO), 1 Tbsp
3. Mozzarella, 2 oz/Cheddar Cheese, 1 oz
4. Medium Chunky Salsa, 4 oz
5. Shrimp (31/40 ct. per lb) butterflied and brushed with GHO & Lemon Juice, 6
6. Seared Steak strips, 1½ oz
7. Grape Tomatoes, 9
8. Red/Yellow Mini Pepper slices, ½ oz
9. Anaheim Chili slices, ½ oz
10. Monterey Jack Cheese, 1 oz
11. Avocado slice/s garnish
12. Cherry Pepper/s garnish

Assembly

1. Form dough into 10 inch round
2. Spread GHO to cover round
3. Spread Mozzarella/Cheddar over GHO
4. Spread Salsa over Cheese
5. Place Shrimp
6. Place Steak slices
7. Place Tomatoes
8. Place Pepper slices
9. Place Chili slices
10. Sprinkle Jack over toppings

    Bake 12–15 minutes at 450 F until bread golden brown and cheese bubbling.

11. Garnish with Avocado slice/s
12. Garnish with Cherry Pepper/s

Steak Fajitas

Toppings

1. Dough recipe of choice, 7 oz.
2. Garlic Herb Oil (GHO), 1 Tbsp
3. Fresh Cilantro to taste
4. Mozzarella Cheese, 2 oz/Cheddar Cheese, 1 oz
5. Medium Chunky Salsa, 4 oz
6. Seared Flank Steak slices, 2 oz
7. Anaheim Chile slices, ½ oz
8. Red/Yellow Mini Pepper slices, ½ oz
9. Red Onion slices, 1 oz
10. Black Olive slices, 1 oz
11. Monterey Jack Cheese, 1 oz
12. Avocado slice/s garnish
13. Cherry Pepper/s garnish

Assembly

1. Form dough into 10 inch round
2. Spread GHO to cover round
3. Sprinkle Cilantro over GHO
4. Spread Mozzarella/Cheddar over GHO
5. Spread Salsa over Cheese
6. Place Steak slices
7. Place Chili slices
8. Place Pepper slices
9. Place Onion slices
10. Place Olive slices
11. Sprinkle Jack over toppings

    Bake 12–15 minutes at 450 F until bread golden brown and cheese bubbling.

12. Garnish with Avocado slice/s
13. Garnish with Cherry Pepper/s

Anchovies - Tomato Sauce - Onion - Capers - Kalamata - Pine Nuts

Toppings

1. Dough recipe of choice, 7 oz
2. Garlic Herb Oil (GHO), 1 Tbsp
3. Smoked Mozzarella Cheese, 3 oz
4. Tomato Sauce, 3 oz
5. Anchovies, 2 oz
6. Grilled Onion slices, 2 oz
7. Pitted Kalamata Olives, 9
8. Capers, ½ oz
9. Pine Nuts, ½ oz
10. Provolone Cheese, 1 oz
11. Basil Sprig garnish

Assembly

1. Form dough into 10 inch round
2. Spread GHO to cover round
3. Spread Mozzarella over GHO
4. Spread Sauce over Cheese
5. Place Anchovies
6. Sprinkle Onion slices over toppings
7. Place Olives
8. Sprinkle Capers over toppings
9. Sprinkle Nuts over toppings
10. Sprinkle Provolone over toppings

    Bake 12–15 minutes at 450 F until bread golden brown and cheese bubbling.

11. Garnish with Basil Sprig

Omelette - Shrimp - Mushroom - Pepper - Bacon - Onion

Toppings

1. Dough recipe of choice, 7 oz
2. Garlic Herb Oil (GHO), 1 Tbsp
3. Fresh Mozzarella Cheese, 3 oz
4. Medium Eggs stirred together, 2
5. Shrimp (31/40 ct. per lb) butterflied and brushed with GHO & Lemon Juice, 8
6. Sautéed Button slices, 1 oz
7. Red/Yellow Mini Pepper slices, ½ oz
8. Green Onion slices, ½ oz
9. Cooked Bacon strips, ½ oz
10. Parmesan Cheese, ½ oz
11. Fresh grated Black Pepper
12. Cherry Pepper/s garnish

Assembly

1. Form dough into 10 inch round
2. Spread GHO to cover round
3. Spread Mozzarella over GHO
4. Pour Eggs over Mozarella
5. Place Shrimp
6. Place Mushroom slices
7. Place Pepper slices
8. Place Onion slices
9. Place Bacon strips
10. Sprinkle Parmesan over toppings
11. Grate Pepper over toppings

   Bake 12–15 minutes at 450 F until bread golden brown and cheese bubbling.

12. Garnish with Cherry Pepper/s

Scallops - Shrimp - Bacon - BBQ Sauce - Pepper - Chili - Pineapple

Toppings

1. Dough recipe of choice, 7 oz.
2. Garlic Herb Oil (GHO), 1 Tbsp
3. Smoked Mozzarella Cheese, 3 oz
4. BBQ Sauce, 2 oz
5. Shrimp (31/40 ct. per lb) butterflied and brushed with BBQ Sauce, 6
6. Scallop slices brushed with BBQ Sauce, 6
7. Cooked Bacon strips, ½ oz
8. Red/Yellow Mini Pepper slices, ½ oz
9. Anaheim Chili slices, ½ oz
10. Grilled Pineapple chunks, 1 ½ oz
11. Monterey Jack Cheese, 1 oz
12. Cherry Pepper/s garnish

Assembly

1. Form dough into 10 inch round
2. Spread GHO to cover round
3. Spread Mozzarella over GHO
4. Drizzle Sauce over Cheese
5. Place Shrimp
6. Place Scallop slices
7. Place Bacon strips
8. Place Pepper slices
9. Place Chili slices
10. Place Pineapple chunks
11. Sprinkle Jack over toppings

   Bake 12–15 minutes at 450 F until bread golden brown and cheese bubbling.

12. Garnish with Cherry Pepper/s

Shrimp - Chicken - Sausage - Anaheim Chili - Onion - Pepper

Toppings

1. Dough recipe of choice, 7 oz
2. Garlic Herb Oil (GHO), 1 Tbsp
3. Fresh Mozzarella Cheese, 3 oz
4. Tomato Sauce, 3 oz
5. Shrimp (31/40 ct. per lb) butterflied and brushed with GHO & Lemon Juice, 6
6. Grilled Chicken strips, 1 oz
7. Sausage crumbles, 1 oz
8. Red/Yellow Mini Pepper slices, ½ oz
9. Anaheim Chili slices, ½ oz
10. Red Onion slices, ½ oz
11. Provolone Cheese, 1 oz
12. Basil sprig garnish
13. Cherry Pepper & Pepperoncini garnish

Assembly

1. Form dough into 10 inch round
2. Spread GHO to cover round
3. Spread Mozzarella over GHO
4. Spread Sauce over Cheese
5. Place Shrimp
6. Place Chicken strips
7. Place Sausage crumbles
8. Place Pepper slices
9. Place Chili slices
10. Sprinkle Onion slices over toppings
11. Sprinkle Provolone over toppings

    Bake 12–15 minutes at 450 F until bread golden brown and cheese bubbling.

12. Garnish with Basil sprig, Cherry Pepper & Pepperoncini

Shrimp - Clam Sauce - Crab - Chilies - Mini Pepper - Leeks

Toppings

1. Dough recipe of choice, 7 oz.
2. Garlic Herb Oil (GHO), 1 Tbsp
3. Mozzarella Cheese, 3 oz
4. Clam Sauce, 4 oz
5. Shrimp (31/40 ct per lb) brushed with GHO & Lemon Juice, 6
6. Crab, 1½ oz
7. Anaheim Chili slices, ½ oz
8. Red/Yellow Mini Pepper slices, ½ oz
9. Leek slices, ½ oz
10. Fontina Cheese, 1 oz
11. Cherry Pepper/s garnish

Assembly

1. Form dough into 10 inch round
2. Spread GHO to cover round
3. Spread Mozzarella over GHO
4. Spread Sauce over Cheese
5. Place Shrimp
6. Place Crab
7. Place Chilies
8. Place Pepper slices
9. Place Leek slices
10. Sprinkle Fontina over toppings

    Bake 12–15 minutes at 450 F until bread golden brown and cheese bubbling.
11. Place Cherry Pepper/s

Shrimp - Clam Sauce - Scallops - Bacon - Mini Pepper

Toppings

1. Dough recipe of choice, 7 oz
2. Garlic Herb Oil (GHO), 1 Tbsp
3. Fresh Mozzarella Cheese, 3 oz
4. Clam Sauce, 4 oz
5. Shrimp (31/40 ct. per lb) brushedwith GHO & Lemon Juice, 6
6. Scallop slices brushed with GHO & Lemon Juice, 6
7. Cooked Bacon strips, ½ oz
8. Anaheim Chili slices, ½ oz
9. Red/Yellow Mini Pepper slices, ½ oz
10. Fontina Cheese, 1 oz
11. Clam/s garnish
12. Mussel/s garnish
13. Lemon wedge garnish

Assembly

1. Form dough into 10 inch round
2. Spread GHO to cover round
3. Spread Mozzarella over GHO
4. Spread Sauce over Cheese
5. Place Shrimp
6. Place Scallop slices
7. Place Bacon strips
8. Place Chili slices
9. Place Pepper slices
10. Sprinkle Fontina over toppings

    Bake 12–15 minutes at 450 F until bread golden brown and cheese bubbling.

11. Garnish with Clams
12. Garnish with Mussels
13. Garnish with Lemon wedge

Shrimp - Squid - Mussels - Octopus - Crab - Mini Pepper

Toppings

1. Dough recipe of choice, 7 oz.
2. Garlic Herb Oil (GHO), 1 Tbsp
3. Fresh Mozzarella Cheese, 3 oz
4. Clam Sauce, 4 oz
5. Shrimp (31/40 ct per lb) brushed with GHO & Lemon Juice, 8
6. Blanched Squid, Mussels, Octopus mix, Crab, 2 oz
7. Red/Yellow Mini Pepper slices, ½ oz
8. Anaheim Chili slices, ½ oz
9. Fontina Cheese, 1 oz
10. Mussel/s garnish
11. Lemon slice/s garnish

Assembly

1. Form dough into 10 inch round
2. Spread GHO to cover round
3. Spread Mozzarella over GHO
4. Spread Sauce over Cheese
5. Place Shrimp

   Place in oven and bake 8 minutes at 450 F, remove and

6. Place Squid, Mussels, Octopus, Crab mix
7. Place Pepper slices
8. Place Chili slices
9. Sprinkle Fontina over toppings and continue baking until bread golden brown and cheese bubbling.
10. Garnish with Mussels
11. Garnish with Lemon slices

Salmon - Cream Cheese - Capers - Red Onion - Cucumbers

Toppings

1. Dough recipe of choice, 7 oz
2. Cream Cheese, 3 oz
3. Seasoned Salmon Filet slices ¼ inch thick, 4 oz
4. Red Onion slices, 1 oz
5. Capers, ½ oz
6. Cucumbers slices, 1½ oz
7. Lemon wedges garnish, 2

Assembly

1. Form dough into 10 inch round
2. Spread Cream Cheese over round
3. Place Salmon slices
4. Sprinkle Onion over Salmon
5. Sprinkle Capers over toppings

   Bake 10–12 minutes at 450 until bread crispy and light golden. Monitor while baking to avoid over cooking Salmon.

6. Place Cucumber slices
7. Garnish with Lemon wedge/s

Shrimp - Crab - Spinach - Sautéed Mushroom - Mini Pepper

Toppings

1. Dough recipe of choice, 7 oz
2. Garlic Herb Oil (GHO), 1 Tbsp
3. Fresh Mozzarella Cheese, 3 oz
4. Clam Sauce, 4 oz
5. Sautéed Spinach, 1 oz
6. Shrimp (31/40 ct. per lb) brushed with GHO & Lemon Juice, 7
7. Crab strips, 1 oz
8. Sautéed Button Mushroom slices, 1 oz
9. Grilled Yellow Mini Pepper slices, 1 oz
10. Fontina Cheese, 1 oz
11. Basil Sprig/s garnish
12. Clam/s garnish
13. Mussel/s garnish

Assembly

1. Form dough into 10 inch round
2. Spread GHO to cover round
3. Spread Mozzarella over GHO
4. Spread Sauce over Cheese
5. Spread Spinach over Sauce
6. Place Shrimp
7. Place Crab strips
8. Place Mushroom slices
9. Place Pepper slices
10. Sprinkle Fontina over toppings

    Bake 12–15 minutes at 450 F until bread golden brown and cheese bubbling.

11. Garnish with Basil Sprig/s
12. Garnish with Clam/s
13. Garnish with Mussel/s

Shrimp - White Sauce - Sautéed Mushroom - Bell Pepper

Toppings

1. Dough recipe of choice, 7 oz
2. Garlic Herb Oil (GHO), 1 Tbsp
3. White Sauce (see recipe), 4 oz
4. Shrimp (31/40 ct. per lb) butterflied, 8
5. Sautéed Button Mushroom slices, 1½ oz
6. Grilled Red/Yellow Bell Pepper strips, 1½ oz

Assembly

1. Form dough into 10 inch round
2. Spread GHO to lightly cover round
3. Place Shrimp, Mushroom slices and Pepper strips in bowl with White Sauce and mix. Empty and spread over round.

   Bake 12–15 minutes at 450 F until bread golden brown and cheese bubbling.

Deep Dish Pizza

Chicken BBQ Caribbean

Toppings

1. Dough recipe of choice, 10 oz
2. Garlic Herb Oil (GHO), 1 Tbsp
3. Smoked Mozzarella Cheese, 4 oz
4. Grilled Chicken strips, 4 oz
5. Red/Yellow Mini Pepper slices, 1 oz
6. Green Bell Pepper slices, 1 oz
7. Grilled Onion slices, 2 oz
8. Medium Chunky Salsa, 4 oz
9. BBQ Sauce, 2 oz
10. Monterey Jack Cheese, 2 oz
11. Grilled Pineapple sliced thin, 6
12. Grilled Mango strips, 2 oz
13. Cherry Pepper/s garnish

Assembly

1. Spread dough in oiled tart pan
2. Spread GHO to lightly cover dough
3. Spread Mozzarella over GHO
4. Place Chicken strips
5. Place Mini Pepper slices
6. Green Bell Pepper slices
7. Place Onion slices
8. Spread Salsa over toppings
9. Drizzle BBQ Sauce over Salsa
10. Sprinkle Jack over toppings
11. Place Pineapple slices over toppings
12. Place Mango strips

    Bake 25–40 minutes at 425 F until surface bubbling.

13. Garnish with Cherry Pepper/s

Broccoli – White Sauce – Sautéed Mushroom – Bell Pepper

Toppings

1. Dough recipe of choice, 10 oz
2. Garlic Herb Oil (GHO), 1 Tbsp
3. White Sauce (see recipe), 5–6 oz
4. Broccoli florets, 2½ oz
5. Sautéed Button/Crimini Mushroom slices, 2½ oz
6. Grilled Red/Yellow Bell Pepper strips, 2½ oz
7. Grilled Yellow Squash slices, 2½ oz
8. Parmesan, 1 oz

Assembly

1. Spread dough in oiled tart pan
2. Spread GHO to lightly cover dough
3. Mix in bowl Sauce, Broccoli florets, Mushroom slices, Pepper strips, Squash and empty/spread over dough.
4. Sprinkle Parmesan over toppings

Bake 25–40 minutes at 425 F until surface bubbling.

Eggplant – Tomato Sauce – Broccoli – Mushroom – Artichoke

Toppings

1. Dough recipe of choice, 10 oz
2. Garlic Herb Oil (GHO), 1 Tbsp
3. Fresh Mozzarella Cheese, 4 oz
4. Goat Cheese, 1 oz
5. Marinated Artichoke Heart wedges, 1½ oz
6. Grilled Red/Yellow Bell Pepper strips, 1½ oz
7. Sautéed Button Mushroom slices, 1½ oz
8. Broccoli florets, 1½ oz
9. Pitted Kalamata Olives, 9
10. Tomato Sauce, 6 oz
11. Fontina Cheese, 2 oz
12. Tomato slice 1, grilled Eggplant slices 3, grilled Yellow Squash slices 3, sautéed Mushroom slices 3
13. Parmesan Cheese, 1 oz

Assembly

1. Spread dough in oiled tart pan
2. Spread GHO to lightly cover dough
3. Spread Mozzarella over GHO
4. Fork Goat Cheese over Cheese
5. Place Artichoke wedges
6. Place Pepper strips
7. Place Mushroom slices
8. Place Broccoli florets
9. Sprinkle Olives over toppings
10. Spread Tomato Sauce over toppings
11. Sprinkle Fontina over toppings
12. Top off with Tomato slice, Eggplant slices, Squash slices, Mushroom slices
13. Sprinkle Parmesan over toppings

Bake 25–40 minutes at 425 F until surface bubbling.

Meatball - Tomato Sauce - Pepper - Mushroom - Onion

Toppings

1. Dough recipe of choice, 10 oz
2. Garlic Herb Oil (GHO), 1 Tbsp
3. Fresh Mozzarella Cheese, 4 oz
4. Meatball quarters, 4 oz
5. Grilled Onion strips, 2 oz
6. Sautéed Crimini Mushroom slices, 2 oz
7. Tomato Sauce, 6 oz
8. Provolone Cheese, 2 oz
9. Green/Red/Yellow Bell Pepper slices, 7
10. Sautéed Crimini Mushroom slices, 7
11. Parmesan Cheese, 1 oz
12. Cherry Pepper/s garnish
13. Basil Sprig garnish

Assembly

1. Spread dough in oiled tart pan
2. Spread GHO to lightly cover dough
3. Spread Mozzarella over GHO
4. Place Meatball quarters
5. Place Onion strips
6. Place Mushroom slices
7. Spread Tomato Sauce over toppings
8. Sprinkle Provolone over toppings
9. Place Pepper slices
10. Place Mushroom slices
11. Sprinkle Parmesan over toppings

   Bake 25–40 minutes at 425 F until surface bubbling.

12. Garnish with Cherry Pepper/s
13. Garnish with Basil Sprig

Pepperoni - Tomato Sauce - Sausage - Pepper - Mushroom

Toppings

1. Dough recipe of choice, 10 oz
2. Garlic Herb Oil (GHO), 1 Tbsp
3. Mozzarella Cheese, 4 oz
4. Sausage crumbles, 2 oz
5. Bell Pepper strips, 2 oz
6. Sautéed Button Mushroom slices, 2 oz
7. Grilled Onion slices, 2 oz
8. Tomato Sauce, 6 oz
9. Provolone Cheese, 2 oz
10. Pepperoni slices, 2 oz
11. Black Olive slices, 1 oz
12. Basil Sprig garnish
13. Cherry Pepper garnish, 1

Assembly

1. Spread dough in oiled tart pan
2. Spread GHO to lightly cover dough
3. Spread Mozzarella over GHO
4. Place Sausage crumbles
5. Place Pepper strips
6. Place Mushroom slices
7. Place Onion slices
8. Spread Sauce over toppings
9. Sprinkle Provolone over toppings
10. Place Pepperoni slices
11. Sprinkle Olive slices over toppings

    Bake 25–40 minutes at 425 F until surface bubbling.

12. Garnish with Basil Sprig
13. Garnish with Cherry Pepper

Pizza Pie Margherita

Toppings

1. Dough recipe of choice, 10 oz
2. Garlic Herb Oil (GHO), 1 Tbsp
3. Fresh Mozzarella Cheese, 6 oz
4. Tomato Sauce, 6 oz
5. Grape Tomatoes, 12
6. Parmesan Cheese, 1 oz
7. Basil Sprig garnish

Assembly

1. Spread dough in oiled tart pan
2. Spread GHO to lightly cover round
3. Spread Cheese over GHO
4. Spread Tomato Sauce over Cheese
5. Place Grape Tomatoes
6. Sprinkle Parmesan over toppings

   Bake 25–30 minutes at 425 F until surface bubbling.

7. Garnish with Basil Sprig

   After baking allow toppings to settle for 5-10 minutes

Pizza Paella

Toppings

1. Dough recipe of choice, 10 oz
2. Garlic Herb Oil (GHO), 1 Tbsp
3. Mozzarella Cheese, 4 oz
4. Sausage crumbles, 2 oz
5. Grilled Chicken strips, 2 oz
6. Shrimp (51/60 ct. per lb) brushed with GHO and Lemon Juice, 6–8
7. Grilled Onion strips, 2 oz
8. Tomato Sauce, 6 oz
9. Provolone Cheese, 2 oz
10. Green/Red/Yellow Bell Pepper slices, 7
11. Cherry Pepper/Basil Sprig garnish

Assembly

1. Spread dough in oiled tart pan
2. Spread GHO to lightly cover dough
3. Spread Mozzarella over GHO
4. Place Sausage crumbles
5. Place Chicken strips
6. Place Shrimp
7. Place Onion strips
8. Spread Tomato Sauce over toppings
9. Sprinkle Provolone over toppings
10. Top off with Pepper slices

    Bake 25–40 minutes at 425 F until surface bubbles.

11. Garnish with Cherry Pepper/Basil Sprig

Salami - Tomato Sauce - Artichoke - Pepper - Mushroom - Olive

Toppings

1. Dough recipe of choice, 10 oz
2. Garlic Herb Oil (GHO), 1 Tbsp
3. Fresh Mozzarella Cheese, 4 oz
4. Goat Cheese, 1 oz
5. Grilled Bell Pepper strips, 2 oz
6. Grilled Button Mushroom slices, 2 oz
7. Marinated Sun Dried Tomatoes julienne, 1 oz
8. Tomato Sauce 6 oz
9. Provolone Cheese, 2 oz
10. Salami slices, 2 oz
11. Marinated Artichoke Heart wedges, 2 oz
12. Black Olive slices, 1 oz
13. Basil Sprig, Cherry Pepper/s, garnish

Assembly

1. Spread dough in oiled tart pan
2. Spread GHO to lightly cover dough
3. Spread Mozzarella over GHO
4. Fork Goat Cheese over Mozzarella
5. Place Pepper strips
6. Place Mushroom slices
7. Place Tomatoes julienne
8. Spread Tomato Sauce over toppings
9. Sprinkle Provolone over toppings
10. Place Salami slices
11. Place Artichoke wedges
12. Sprinkle Olive slices over toppings

Bake 25–40 minutes at 425 F until surface bubbling.

13. Garnish with Basil Sprig & Cherry Pepper/s

Zucchini - Asparagus - Broccoli - Bell Pepper - Mushroom - Olive

Toppings

1. Dough recipe of choice, 10 oz
2. Garlic Herb Oil (GHO), 1 Tbsp
3. Fresh Mozzarella Cheese, 4 oz
4. Broccoli florets, 1½ oz
5. Sautéed Button Mushroom slices, 1½ oz
6. Grilled Bell Pepper strips, 1½ oz
7. Tomato Sauce, 6 oz
8. Fontina Cheese, 2 oz
9. Asparagus spears, 2 oz
10. Grilled Zucchini strips, 2 oz
11. Black Olive slices, 1 oz
12. Parmesan Cheese, 1 oz
13. Basil Sprig garnish

Assembly

1. Spread dough in oiled tart pan
2. Spread GHO to lightly cover dough
3. Spread Mozzarella over GHO
4. Place Broccoli florets
5. Place Mushroom slices
6. Place Pepper strips
7. Spread Tomato Sauce over toppings
8. Sprinkle Fontina over toppings
9. Place Asparagus spears
10. Place Zucchini strips
11. Sprinkle Olive slices over toppings
12. Sprinkle Parmesan over toppings

    Bake 25–40 minutes at 425 F until surface bubbling.

13. Garnish with Basil Sprig

Flatbread Sandwiches

Flatbread sandwiches are perfect for utilizing your leftover pizza toppings. You will miss out on the fun but spare yourself the time and effort involved in making the pizza dough, while at the same time appeasing your hunger for pizza with a tasty substitute.

The sandwiches featured here utilize many of the same toppings that you put on your pizza. Most any topping you place on a pizza you can put on a baguette, French roll, ciabatta or a thick slice of Italian bread. Brush or spread a layer of garlic herb oil over the bread before placing the toppings. This adds flavor and helps prevent sauce absorption into the bread. You can use the same tomato sauce you use for your pizza or select a sauce of your choosing. For instance you may choose to substitute pesto for the tomato sauce. Select toppings that marry well with your sauce.

Flatbread sandwiches can be assembled with or without cheese. Use sliced cheese to top off the sandwiches that complement the toppings. Cheese adds flavor and facilitates holding the toppings in place while baking and eating. Any good melting cheese used on pizza can be used to top off your sandwich.

Prepare the toppings as you would for pizza. Portion and make substitutions, deletions and additions with the toppings that please your palate. Less is sometimes preferable to more and you can limit the toppings as desired.

Prior to baking preheat the oven. Place sandwiches directly on your pizza stone or the oven's grills. Bake the sandwiches for 12–15 minutes at 450 degrees until the cheese is melted and just starting to lightly brown and the bread is crispy. Oven types and temperatures vary, so be sure to monitor the sandwiches during baking. An electric toaster oven is convenient when available to eliminate the necessity of preheating the oven.

Bon appétit!

Grilled Chicken Caribbean BBQ

Toppings

1. Baguette or French Roll, 8 oz
2. Garlic Herb Oil (GHO), 1 Tbsp
3. Fresh Cilantro
4. Grilled Chicken strips brushed with BBQ Sauce
5. Red/Orange Mini Pepper slices
6. Red Onion slices
7. Grilled Pineapple chunks
8. Grilled Mango strips
9. BBQ Sauce, ½–1 oz
10. Smoked Gouda Cheese slice, 1 oz

Assembly

1. Slice Baguette or French Roll in half
2. Spread GHO to lightly cover bread surface
3. Portion and place toppings as desired
4. Drizzle Sauce over toppings
5. Top with Gouda slice

Bake 12–15 minutes at 450 F until bread crispy and cheese melted and starting to brown.

Shrimp Caribbean BBQ

Toppings

1. Baguette or French Roll, 8 oz
2. Garlic Herb Oil (GHO), 1 Tbsp
3. Fresh Cilantro
4. Shrimp (31/40 ct. per lb) butterflied & brushed with BBQ Sauce
5. Red & Orange Mini Pepper slices
6. Red Onion slices
7. Grilled Pineapple chunks
8. Grilled Mango strips
9. BBQ Sauce, ½–1 oz
10. Smoked Mozzarella Cheese slice, 1 oz

Assembly

1. Slice Baguette or French Roll in half
2. Spread GHO to lightly cover bread surface
3. Portion and place toppings as desired
4. Drizzle Sauce over toppings
5. Top with Mozzarella slice

Bake 12–15 minutes at 450 F until bread crispy and cheese melted and starting to brown.

Mango Pork BBQ

Ham - Onion - Pepper - Pineapple

Toppings

1. Baguette or French Roll, 8 oz
2. Garlic Herb Oil (GHO), 1 Tbsp
3. Fresh Cilantro
4. Roasted shredded Pork brushed with BBQ Sauce
5. Red/Orange Mini Pepper slices
6. Red Onion slices
7. Grilled Pineapple chunks
8. Grilled Mango strips
9. BBQ Sauce, ½–1 oz
10. Smoked Gouda Cheese slice, 1 oz

Toppings

1. Baguette or French Roll, 8 oz
2. Garlic Herb Oil (GHO), 1 Tbsp
3. Tomato Sauce, ½ –1 oz
4. Ham slices
5. Onion slices
6. Green/Red Bell Pepper strips
7. Grilled Pineapple chunks
8. Provolone Cheese slice, 1 oz

Assembly

1. Slice Baguette or French Roll in half
2. Spread GHO to lightly cover bread surface
3. Portion and place toppings as desired
4. Drizzle Sauce over toppings
5. Top with Gouda slice

   Bake 12–15 minutes at 450 F until bread crispy and cheese melted and starting to brown.

Assembly

1. Slice Baguette or French Roll in half
2. Spread GHO to lightly cover bread surface
3. Spread Sauce over toppings
4. Portion and place toppings as desired
5. Top with Provolone slice

   Bake 12–15 minutes at 450 F until bread crispy and cheese melted and starting to brown.

Artichoke - Broccoli - Squash - Tomato

Toppings

1. Baguette or French Roll, 8 oz
2. Garlic Herb Oil (GHO), 1 Tbsp
3. Tomato Sauce, ½ - 1 oz
4. Marinated Artichoke Heart quarters
5. Broccoli florets
6. Grilled Yellow Squash strips
7. Grilled Zucchini strips
8. Sautéed mushrooms slices
9. Marinated Sun Dried Tomatoes julienne
10. Black Olive slices
11. Provolone Cheese slice, 1 oz

Assembly

1. Slice Baguette or French Roll in half
2. Spread GHO to lightly cover bread surface
3. Spread Sauce over GHO
4. Portion and place toppings as desired
5. Top with Provolone slice

   Bake 12–15 minutes at 450 F until bread crispy and cheese melted and starting to brown.

Artichoke - Mushroom - Pepper

Toppings

1. Baguette or French Roll, 8 oz
2. Garlic Herb Oil (GHO), 1 Tbsp
3. Tomato Sauce, ½–1 oz
4. Goat Cheese
5. Marinated Artichoke Heart quarters
6. Sautéed Mushroom slices
7. Broccoli florets
8. Red/Yellow Mini Pepper rings
9. Marinated Sun Dried Tomatoes julienne
10. Black Olive slices
11. Provolone Cheese slice, 1 oz

Assembly

1. Slice Baguette or French Roll in half
2. Spread GHO to lightly cover bread surface
3. Spread Sauce over GHO
4. Portion and place toppings as desired
5. Top with Provolone slice

   Bake 12–15 minutes at 450 F until bread crispy and Cheese melted and starting to brown.

Artichoke - Mushroom - Mini Pepper

Asparagus - Grilled Squash - Tomato

Toppings

1. Baguette or French Roll, 8 oz
2. Garlic Herb Oil (GHO), 1 Tbsp
3. Tomato Sauce, ½–1 oz
4. Marinated Artichoke Heart quarters
5. Sautéed Mushroom slices
6. Grilled Mini Pepper strips
7. Goat Cheese crumbles
8. Provolone Cheese slice, 1 oz

Toppings

1. Baguette or French Roll, 8 oz
2. Garlic Herb Oil (GHO), 1 Tbsp
3. Tomato Sauce, ½–1 oz
4. Asparagus tips
5. Grilled Yellow Squash strips
6. Marinated Sun Dried Tomato julienne
7. Provolone Cheese Slice, 1 oz

Assembly

1. Slice Baguette or French Roll in half
2. Spread GHO to lightly cover bread surface
3. Spread Sauce over toppings
4. Portion and place toppings as desired
5. Top with Provolone slice

   Bake 12–15 minutes at 450 F until bread crispy and cheese melted and starting to brown.

Assembly

1. Slice Baguette or French Roll in half
2. Spread GHO to lightly cover bread surface
3. Spread Sauce over toppings
4. Portion and place toppings as desired
5. Top with Provolone slice

   Bake 12–15 minutes at 450 F until bread crispy and cheese melted and starting to brown.

Asparagus - Squash - Mushroom

Toppings

1. Baguette or French Roll, 8 oz
2. Garlic Herb Oil (GHO), 1 Tbsp
3. Tomato Sauce, ½–1 oz
4. Asparagus tips
5. Grilled Yellow Squash strips
6. Grilled Zucchini strips
7. Sautéed Mushroom slices
8. Marinated Sun Dried Tomatoes julienne
9. Black Olive slices
10. Provolone Cheese slice, 1 oz

Assembly

1. Slice Baguette or French Roll in half
2. Spread GHO to lightly cover bread surface
3. Spread Sauce over toppings
4. Portion and place toppings as desired
5. Top with Provolone slice

   Bake 12–15 minutes at 450 F until bread crispy and cheese melted and starting to brown.

Asparagus - Mushroom - Mini Pepper

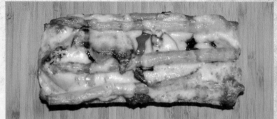

Toppings

1. Baguette or French Roll, 8 oz
2. Garlic Herb Oil (GHO), 1 Tbsp
3. Tomato Sauce, ½–1 oz
4. Asparagus tips
5. Sautéed Mushroom slices
6. Grilled Mini Pepper strips
7. Provolone Cheese slice, 1 oz

Assembly

1. Slice Baguette or French Roll in half
2. Spread GHO to lightly cover bread surface
3. Spread Sauce over toppings
4. Portion and place toppings as desired
5. Top with Provolone slice

   Bake 12–15 minutes at 450 F until bread crispy and cheese melted and starting to brown.

Broccoli-Mushroom-Artichoke-Olive

Toppings

1. Baguette or French Roll, 8 oz
2. Garlic Herb Oil (GHO), 1 Tbsp
3. Tomato Sauce, ½–1 oz
4. Broccoli florets
5. Sautéed Mushroom slices
6. Marinated Artichoke Heart quarters
7. Kalamata Olive halves
8. Provolone Cheese slice, 1 oz

Assembly

1. Slice Baguette or French Roll in half
2. Spread GHO to lightly cover bread surface
3. Spread Sauce over toppings
4. Portion and place toppings as desired
5. Top with Provolone slice

   Bake 12–15 minutes at 450 F until bread crispy and cheese melted and starting to brown.

Broccoli-Mushroom-Pepper-Tomato

Toppings

1. Baguette or French Roll, 8 oz
2. Garlic Herb Oil (GHO), 1 Tbsp
3. Tomato Sauce, ½–1 oz
4. Sautéed Mushroom slices
5. Broccoli florets
6. Grilled Mini Pepper strips
7. Marinated Sun Dried Tomato julienne
8. Provolone Cheese slice, 1 oz

Assembly

1. Slice Baguette or French Roll in half
2. Spread GHO to lightly cover bread surface
3. Spread Sauce over toppings
4. Portion and place toppings as desired
5. Top with Provolone slice

   Bake 12–15 minutes at 450 F until bread crispy and cheese melted and starting to brown.

Mushroom - Goat Cheese - Mini Pepper

Pepper - Mushroom - Onion - Tomato

Toppings

1. Baguette or French Roll, 8 oz
2. Garlic Herb Oil (GHO), 1 Tbsp
3. Tomato Sauce, ½–1 oz
4. Goat Cheese
5. Sautéed Mushroom slices
6. Grilled Mini Pepper strips
7. Provolone Cheese slice, 1 oz

Toppings

1. Baguette or French Roll, 8 oz
2. Garlic Herb Oil (GHO), 1 Tbsp
3. Tomato Sauce, ½–1 oz
4. Goat Cheese
5. Sautéed Mushroom slices
6. Grilled Orange Bell Pepper strips
7. Red Onion slices
8. Marinated Sun Dried Tomato julienne
9. Provolone Cheese slice, 1 oz

Assembly

1. Slice Baguette or French Roll in half
2. Spread GHO to lightly cover bread surface
3. Spread Sauce over toppings
4. Fork Goat Cheese over toppings
5. Portion and place toppings as desired
6. Top with Provolone slice

   Bake 12–15 minutes at 450 F until bread crispy and cheese melted and starting to brown.

Assembly

1. Slice Baguette or French Roll in half
2. Spread GHO to lightly cover bread surface
3. Spread Sauce over toppings
4. Fork Goat Cheese over toppings
5. Portion and place toppings as desired
6. Top with Provolone slice

   Bake 12–15 minutes at 450 F until bread crispy and cheese melted and starting to brown.

Red Onion - Mushroom - Mini Pepper

Eggplant - Mushroom - Pepper - Tomato

Toppings

1. Baguette or French Roll, 8 oz
2. Garlic Herb Oil (GHO), 1 Tbsp
3. Tomato Sauce, ½–1 oz
4. Goat Cheese
5. Red Onion slices
6. Sautéed Mushroom slices
7. Grilled Mini Pepper strips
8. Provolone Cheese slice, 1 oz

Toppings

1. Baguette or French Roll, 8 oz
2. Garlic Herb Oil (GHO), 1 Tbsp
3. Tomato Sauce, ½–1 oz
4. Grilled Japanese Eggplant slices
5. Grilled Yellow Squash slices
6. Sautéed Mushroom slices
7. Red/Yellow/Orange Mini Pepper rings
8. Marinated Sun Dried Tomatoes julienne
9. Provolone Cheese slice, 1 oz

Assembly

1. Slice Baguette or French Roll in half
2. Spread GHO to lightly cover bread surface
3. Spread Sauce over toppings
4. Fork Goat Cheese over toppings
5. Portion and place toppings as desired
6. Top with Provolone slice

   Bake 12–15 minutes at 450 F until bread crispy and cheese melted and starting to brown.

Assembly

1. Slice Baguette or French Roll in half
2. Spread GHO to lightly cover bread surface
3. Spread Sauce over toppings
4. Portion and place toppings as desired
5. Top with Provolone slice

   Bake 12–15 minutes at 450 F until bread crispy and cheese melted and starting to brown.

Squash - Mushroom - Mini Pepper

Toppings

1. Baguette or French Roll, 8 oz
2. Garlic Herb Oil (GHO), 1 Tbsp
3. Tomato Sauce, ½–1 oz
4. Grilled Yellow Squash strips
5. Sautéed Mushroom slices
6. Red/Orange Mini Pepper strips
7. Provolone Cheese slice, 1 oz

Assembly

1. Slice Baguette or French Roll in half
2. Spread GHO to lightly cover bread surface
3. Spread Sauce over toppings
4. Portion and place toppings as desired
5. Top with Provolone slice

   Bake 12–5 minutes at 450 F until bread crispy and cheese melted and starting to brown.

Zucchini - Mushroom - Bell Pepper

Toppings

1. Baguette or French Roll, 8 oz
2. Garlic Herb Oil (GHO), 1 Tbsp
3. Tomato Sauce, ½–1 oz
4. Grilled Zucchini strips
5. Sautéed Mushroom slices
6. Grilled Mini Pepper strips
7. Provolone Cheese slice, 1 oz

Assembly

1. Slice Baguette or French Roll in half
2. Spread GHO to lightly cover bread surface
3. Spread Sauce over toppings
4. Portion and place toppings as desired
5. Top with Provolone slice

   Bake 12–15 minutes at 450 F until bread crispy and cheese melted and starting to brown.

Squash-Tomato-Mushroom-Pepper

Grilled Squash - Asparagus

Toppings

1. Baguette or French Roll, 8 oz
2. Garlic Herb Oil (GHO), 1 Tbsp
3. Tomato Sauce, ½–1 oz
4. Goat Cheese
5. Grilled Yellow Squash slices
6. Grilled Orange Bell Pepper strips
7. Sautéed Mushroom slices
8. Marinated Sun Dried Tomato julienne
9. Provolone Cheese slice, 1 oz

Toppings

1. Baguette or French Roll, 8 oz
2. Garlic Herb Oil (GHO), 1 Tbsp
3. Tomato Sauce, ½–1 oz
4. Grilled Yellow Squash strips
5. Asparagus tips
6. Provolone Cheese, 1 oz

Assembly

1. Slice Baguette or French Roll in half
2. Spread GHO to lightly cover bread surface
3. Spread Sauce over toppings
4. Fork Goat Cheese over toppings
5. Portion and place toppings as desired
6. Top with Provolone slice

   Bake 12–5 minutes at 450 F until bread crispy and cheese melted and starting to brown.

Assembly

1. Slice Baguette or French Roll in half
2. Spread GHO to lightly cover bread surface
3. Spread Sauce over toppings
4. Portion and place toppings as desired
5. Top with Provolone slice

   Bake 12–15 minutes at 450 F until bread crispy and cheese melted and starting to brown.

Tomato - Artichoke - Pepper - Olive

Toppings

1. Baguette or French Roll, 8 oz
2. Garlic Herb Oil (GHO), 1 Tbsp
3. Tomato Sauce, ½–1 oz
4. Goat Cheese
5. Tomato slices
6. Marinated Artichoke Heart quarters
7. Yellow Mini Pepper slices
8. Black Olive slices
9. Provolone Cheese slices 1 oz

Assembly

1. Slice Baguette or French Roll in half
2. Spread GHO to lightly cover bread surface
3. Spread Sauce over toppings
4. Fork Goat Cheese over Tomato Sauce
5. Portion and place toppings as desired
6. Top with Provolone slice

   Bake 12–15 minutes at 450 F until bread crispy and cheese melted and starting to brown.

Zucchini - Asparagus - Mushroom

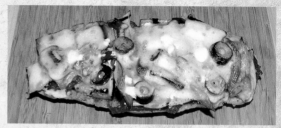

Toppings

1. Baguette or French Roll, 8 oz
2. Garlic Herb Oil (GHO), 1 Tbsp
3. Tomato Sauce, ½–1 oz
4. Goat Cheese
5. Grilled Zucchini strips
6. Asparagus tips
7. Sautéed Mushroom slices
8. Marinated Sun Dried Tomatoes julienne
9. Black Olive slices
10. Provolone, 1 oz

Assembly

1. Slice Baguette or French Roll in half
2. Spread GHO to lightly cover bread surface
3. Spread Sauce over toppings
4. Fork Goat Cheese over toppings
5. Portion and place toppings as desired
6. Top with Provolone slice

   Bake 12–15 minutes at 450 F until bread crispy and cheese melted and starting to brown.

Ham - Asparagus

Toppings

1. Baguette or French Roll, 8 oz
2. Garlic Herb Oil (GHO), 1 Tbsp
3. Tomato Sauce, ½–1 oz
4. Ham slices
5. Asparagus tips
6. Fontina Cheese slice, 1 oz

Assembly

1. Slice Baguette or French Roll in half
2. Spread GHO to lightly cover bread surface
3. Spread Sauce over toppings
4. Portion and place toppings as desired
5. Top with Fontina slice

   Bake 12–15 minutes at 450 F until bread crispy and cheese melted and starting to brown.

Chicken - Artichoke - Mushroom - Pepper

Toppings

1. Baguette or French Roll, 8 oz
2. Garlic Herb Oil (GHO), 1 Tbsp
3. Tomato Sauce, ½–1 oz
4. Grilled Chicken strips
5. Marinated Artichoke Heart quarters
6. Sautéed Mushroom slices
7. Red/Yellow Mini Pepper slices
8. Provolone Cheese slice, 1 oz

Assembly

1. Slice Baguette or French Roll in half
2. Spread GHO to lightly cover bread surface
3. Spread Sauce over toppings
4. Portion and place toppings as desired
5. Top with Provolone slice

   Bake 12–15 minutes at 450 F until bread crispy and cheese melted and starting to brown.

Ham - Artichoke - Mushroom - Olive

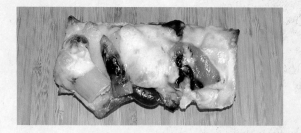

Toppings

1. Baguette or French Roll, 8 oz
2. Garlic Herb Oil (GHO), 1 Tbsp
3. Tomato Sauce, ½–1 oz
4. Ham slices
5. Marinated Artichoke Heart quarters
6. Sautéed Mushroom slices
7. Kalamata Olive halves
8. Provolone Cheese slice, 1 oz

Assembly

1. Slice Baguette or French Roll in half
2. Spread GHO to lightly cover bread surface
3. Spread Sauce over toppings
4. Portion and place toppings as desired
5. Top with Provolone slice

   Bake 12–15 minutes at 450 F until bread crispy and cheese melted and starting to brown.

Pepperoni - Onion - Pepper - Olive

Toppings

1. Baguette or French Roll, 8 oz
2. Garlic Herb Oil (GHO), 1 Tbsp
3. Tomato Sauce, ½–1 oz
4. Traditional Pepperoni slices
5. Red/Yellow Mini peppers slices
6. Green Bell Pepper slices
7. Red Onion tidbits
8. Black Olive slices
9. Provolone Cheese slice, 1 oz

Assembly

1. Slice Baguette or French Roll in half
2. Spread GHO to lightly cover bread surface
3. Spread Sauce over toppings
4. Portion and place toppings as desired
5. Top with Provolone slice

   Bake 12–15 minutes at 450 F until bread crispy and cheese melted and starting to brown.

Pepperoni-Sausage-Pepper-Olive

Toppings

1. Baguette or French Roll, 8 oz
2. Garlic Herb Oil (GHO), 1 Tbsp
3. Tomato Sauce, ½–1 oz
4. Traditional Pepperoni slices
5. Italian Sausage crumbles
6. Red/Yellow Mini Pepper slices
7. Green Bell Pepper slices
8. Red Onion tidbits
9. Black Olive slices
10. Provolone Cheese slice, 1 oz

Assembly

1. Slice Baguette or French Roll in half
2. Spread GHO to lightly cover bread surface
3. Spread Sauce over toppings
4. Portion and place toppings as desired
5. Top with Provolone slice

   Bake 12–5 minutes at 450 F until bread crispy and cheese melted and starting to brown.

Pepperoni-Mushroom-Peppers-Olive

Toppings

1. Baguette or French Roll, 8 oz
2. Garlic Herb Oil (GHO), 1 Tbsp
3. Tomato Sauce, ½–1 oz
4. Traditional Pepperoni slices
5. Sautéed Mushroom slices
6. Red/Yellow Mini Pepper slices
7. Green Bell Pepper slices
8. Black Olive slices
9. Provolone Cheese slice, 1 oz

Assembly

1. Slice Baguette or French Roll in half
2. Spread GHO to lightly cover bread surface
3. Spread Sauce over toppings
4. Portion and place toppings as desired
5. Top with Provolone slice

   Bake 12–15 minutes at 450 F until bread crispy and cheese melted and starting to brown.

Salami-Artichoke-Mushroom-Pepper

Salami-Mushroom-Peppers-Olive

Toppings

1. Baguette or French Roll, 8 oz
2. Garlic Herb Oil (GHO), 1 Tbsp
3. Tomato Sauce, ½–1 oz
4. Goat Cheese
5. Salami slices
6. Marinated Artichoke Heart quarters
7. Red/Yellow Mini Pepper slices
8. Sautéed Mushroom slices
9. Provolone Cheese slice, 1 oz

Toppings

1. Baguette or French Roll, 8 oz
2. Garlic Herb Oil (GHO), 1 Tbsp
3. Tomato Sauce, ½–1 oz
4. Salami slices
5. Sautéed Mushroom slices
6. Red/Yellow Mini Pepper slices
7. Green Bell Pepper slices
8. Black Olive slices
9. Provolone Cheese slice, 1 oz

Assembly

1. Slice Baguette or French Roll in half
2. Spread GHO to lightly cover bread surface
3. Spread Sauce over toppings
4. Fork Goat Cheese over toppings
5. Portion and place toppings as desired
6. Top with Provolone slice

   Bake 12–15 minutes at 450 F until bread crispy and cheese melted and starting to brown.

Assembly

1. Slice Baguette or French Roll in half
2. Spread GHO to lightly cover bread surface
3. Spread Sauce over toppings
4. Portion and place toppings as desired
5. Top with Provolone slice

   Bake 12–5 minutes at 450 F until bread crispy and cheese melted and starting to brown.

Bacon - Tomato - Avocado - Pepper

Toppings

1. Baguette or French Roll, 8 oz
2. Garlic Herb Oil (GHO), 1 Tbsp
3. Tomato Sauce, ½–1 oz
4. Cooked Bacon strips
5. Tomato slices
6. Avocado slices
7. Grilled Yellow Bell Pepper slices
8. Goat Cheese crumbles
9. Black Olive slices
10. Provolone Cheese slice, 1 oz

Assembly

1. Slice Baguette or French Roll in half
2. Spread GHO to lightly cover bread surface
3. Spread Sauce over toppings
4. Portion and place toppings as desired
5. Top with Provolone slice

   Bake 12–15 minutes at 450 F until bread crispy and cheese melted and starting to brown.

Carnitas Santa Fe

Toppings

1. Baguette or French Roll, 8 oz
2. Garlic Herb Oil (GHO), 1 Tbsp
3. Medium Chunky Salsa, ½–1 oz
4. Roasted Pork shredded
5. Red/Yellow Mini Pepper slices
6. Anaheim Chili slices
7. Black Bean/Whole Kernel Corn mix
8. Red Onion slices
9. Black Olive slices
10. Avocado slices
11. Monterey Jack Cheese slice, 1 oz

Assembly

1. Slice Baguette or French Roll in half
2. Spread GHO to lightly cover bread surface
3. Spread Salsa over toppings
4. Portion and place toppings as desired
5. Top with Jack slice

   Bake 12–15 minutes at 450 F until bread crispy and cheese melted and starting to brown.

Grilled Chicken Fajitas Santa Fe

Toppings

1. Baguette or French Roll, 8 oz
2. Garlic Herb Oil (GHO), 1 Tbsp
3. Medium Chunky Salsa, ½–1 oz
4. Fresh Cilantro
5. Grilled Chicken strips
6. Red/Yellow Mini Pepper slices
7. Anaheim Chili slices
8. Black Bean/Whole Kernel Corn mix
9. Red Onion slices
10. Black Olive slices
11. Avocado slices
12. Monterey Jack Cheese slice, 1 oz

Assembly

1. Slice Baguette or French Roll in half
2. Spread GHO to lightly cover bread surface
3. Spread Salsa over toppings
4. Portion and place toppings as desired
5. Top with Jack slice

   Bake 12–15 minutes at 450 F until bread crispy and cheese melted and starting to brown.

Grilled Chicken Rancho BBQ

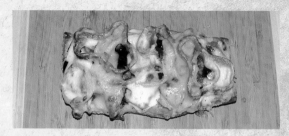

Toppings

1. Baguette or French Roll, 8 oz
2. Garlic Herb Oil (GHO), 1 Tbsp
3. Fresh Cilantro
4. Grilled Chicken strips
5. Bacon strips
6. Red/Yellow Mini Pepper slices
7. Anaheim Chili slices
8. Red Onion slices
9. BBQ Sauce, ½–1 oz
10. Monterey Jack Cheese slice, ½ oz
11. Cheddar Cheese slice, ½ oz

Assembly

1. Slice Baguette or French Roll in half
2. Spread GHO to lightly cover bread surface
3. Portion and place toppings as desired
4. Drizzle Sauce over toppings
5. Top with Jack/Cheddar slices

   Bake 12–15 minutes at 450 F until bread crispy and cheese melted and starting to brown.

Shrimp Fajitas Santa Fe

Toppings

1. Baguette or French Roll, 8 oz
2. Garlic Herb Oil (GHO), 1 Tbsp
3. Salsa, ½–1 oz
4. Fresh Cilantro
5. Shrimp (31/40 ct. per lb) butterflied an-brushed with GHO & Lemon Juice
6. Red/Yellow Mini Pepper slices
7. Anaheim Chili slices
8. Black Bean/Whole Kernel Corn mix
9. Red Onion slices
10. Black Olive slices
11. Avocado slices
12. Monterey Jack Cheese slice, 1 oz

Assembly

1. Slice Baguette or French Roll in half
2. Spread GHO to lightly cover bread surface
3. Spread Salsa over toppings
4. Portion and place toppings as desired
5. Top with Jack slice

   Bake 12–15 minutes at 450 F until bread crispy and cheese melted and starting to brown.

Shrimp Rancho BBQ

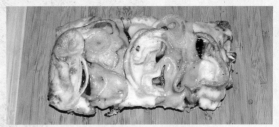

Toppings

1. Baguette or French Roll, 8 oz
2. Garlic Herb Oil (GHO), 1 Tbsp
3. Fresh Cilantro
4. Shrimp (31/40 ct. per lb) butterflied and-brushed with BBQ Sauce
5. Cooked Bacon strips
6. Red/Yellow Mini Pepper slices
7. Anaheim Chili slices
8. Red Onion slices
9. BBQ Sauce, ½–1 oz
10. Monterey Jack Cheese slice ½ oz
11. Cheddar Cheese slice, ½ oz

Assembly

1. Slice Baguette or French Roll in half
2. Spread GHO to lightly cover bread surface
3. Portion and place toppings as desired
4. Drizzle Sauce over toppings
5. Top with Jack/Cheddar slices

   Bake 12–15 minutes at 450 F until bread crispy and cheese melted and starting to brown.

Index

Pizza and Flatbread Recipe Index

Thin Crust Pizza Recipes

Farmhouse Rustico

Deep Dish Pizza Recipes

Flatbread Sandwich Recipes